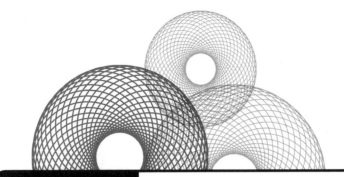

LIVING
with
ANXIETY
DISORDERS

Also in the Teen's Guides series

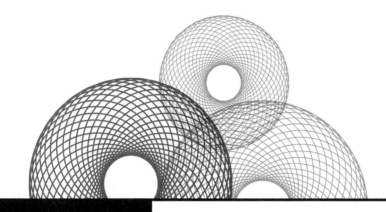

LIVING
with
ANXIETY
DISORDERS

Allen R. Miller, Ph.D.

Facts On File
An imprint of Infobase Publishing

Living with Anxiety Disorders

Copyright © 2008 by Allen R. Miller, Ph.D.

All rights reserved. No part of this book may be reproduced or utilized in any form or by any means, electronic or mechanical, including photocopying, recording, or by any information storage or retrieval systems, without permission in writing from the publisher. For information contact:

Facts On File, Inc.
An imprint of Infobase Publishing
132 West 31st Street
New York NY 10001

Library of Congress Cataloging-in-Publication Data
Miller, Allen R.
  Living with anxiety disorders / by Allen R. Miller.
    p. cm.—(Teen's guides)
  Includes index.
  ISBN-13: 978-0-8160-6344-4
  ISBN-10: 0-8160-6344-3
  1. Anxiety in adolescence. 2. Anxiety disorders. I. Title.
  RJ506.A58M55 2007
  618.92'8522—dc22   2007000553

Facts On File books are available at special discounts when purchased in bulk quantities for businesses, associations, institutions, or sales promotions. Please call our Special Sales Department in New York at (212) 967-8800 or (800) 322-8755.

You can find Facts On File on the World Wide Web at http://www.factsonfile.com

Text design by Annie O'Donnell
Cover design by Joo Young An

Printed in the United States of America

Sheridan CGI 10 9 8 7 6 5 4 3 2 1

This book is printed on acid-free paper.

CONTENTS

Fear v. Anxiety Disorder: What's the Difference?

Karla is a 10th grader who's active in student council, her church, and her school's lacrosse team. But Karla has a secret she tries to hide from everybody, including her closest friends and family. Each morning, Karla takes a long shower and then spends another 30 minutes washing her hands before breakfast. She wants to stop, but her hands just don't feel clean enough, and she can't bring herself to turn off the water. After breakfast she washes again; in fact, it often takes her so long to get ready that she has to rush to get to school on time. At school she tries not to touch doorknobs or handrails, because she's scared she'll catch a serious disease.

During a quiz she checks and rechecks every answer and erases anything that isn't perfectly straight or neat. Sometimes she erases so hard she tears the paper. She worries that if her work isn't perfect something terrible may happen. But with all this checking and fixing she never finishes a test before the time is up.

Karla hides her habits so that others won't think she's weird. She knows that if she weren't washing and cleaning she could have fun with friends or do her schoolwork, but she can't stop herself.

Karla has a type of anxiety problem known as obsessive-compulsive disorder (OCD)—one of six kinds of anxiety disorders discussed in this book. Unfortunately, her situation is not unique. If you've made it through middle school, you know just how anxiety-provoking adolescence can be even on a good day. But in addition to normal anxiety and stress, teens can suffer from anxiety disorders just like adults.

INSTINCTUAL FEAR V. ANXIETY DISORDER

Instinctual fear and anxiety are a normal part of life that can protect and even stimulate you, whether it's a feeling of nervousness before giving a speech or a shiver of fear as you walk down a dark street. But more than 19 million Americans experience far more than just normal anxiety. Instead, their lives are filled with crippling anxiety and fear.

So what's the difference between normal instinctual fear and an anxiety disorder? *Instinctual fear* is a reaction to an actual danger signal. It involves physical and mental tension that helps you spring into action to protect yourself from something scary or dangerous that's about to happen. Once the danger has passed, the fear goes away. The body's reaction to danger is called the *fight-or-flight* response. When you're scared, you can feel your heart start to pound, your stomach tightens, and you breathe faster. All these changes are designed to help you meet a deadly challenge by either fighting or running away. Your heart beats faster so it can pump more blood to your muscles and brain. Your lungs breathe in air more quickly to supply your body with oxygen. The pupils in your eyes widen so you can see better. And your digestive system slows down so you can concentrate on the danger. It's a response that developed in humans thousands of years ago when physical dangers were a constant threat. The caveman who was able to outrun or outfight a saber-toothed tiger lived to tell the tale and pass on his superior fight-or-flight genes to his descendants.

The physical and mental tension of *anxiety* is similar to fear, but with anxiety, there isn't usually any actual danger to trigger the feeling. The feeling comes from the anticipation of future danger—the concern that something bad could happen—and the worry that one doesn't have what it takes to deal with it. Usually your body switches into fight-or-flight mode only when there's something to fear. When you feel scared without real danger, that's called anxiety.

Here's the difference: If a bully takes a swing at you and you feel a burst of energy as you jump back out of the way, that's instinctual fear. If you see a classmate in the distance and your heart starts to pound and waves of terror sweep over you because he looks like someone who might be a bully, that's anxiety.

Psychologists have defined the boundaries between ordinary instinctual fear and anxiety disorders, and this book will help you understand that difference. Although each anxiety disorder has unique features, all anxiety disorders are united by a common theme of excessive fear and dread in the absence of evidence of clear danger. If you have developed a pattern of experiencing too much anxiety on a daily basis, you may be diagnosed with an anxiety disorder.

Tormented by panic attacks, obsessive thoughts, flashbacks of traumatic events, nightmares, or frightening physical symptoms, teens with anxiety disorders may become overwhelmed by their anxieties and eventually feel so frightened that they can't leave the house. You may know someone with an anxiety disorder, or perhaps you're struggling with this problem yourself.

If you are, you're not alone. Anxiety disorders affect as many as one of every eight teens of every age, color, religion, and economic status. They also affect more girls than guys. In fact, anxiety disorders are the most common mental health problem in the United States.

There are six types of anxiety disorders, and many of their symptoms overlap. They include

> ➤ *generalized anxiety disorder (GAD):* This problem causes constant, exaggerated worrisome thoughts and tension about everyday life events and activities. With GAD, you may almost always anticipate the worst although there is little reason to expect it; there also may be physical symptoms such as fatigue, trembling, muscle tension, headache, or nausea.
> ➤ *post-traumatic stress disorder (PTSD):* Experiencing a traumatic event such as an assault, a car accident, or a natural disaster can later trigger a series of symptoms, including irritability, numbed or lack of emotions, nightmares, flashbacks, depression, or anger. Family members of victims also can develop this disorder.
> ➤ *panic disorder:* This problem causes repeated episodes of intense fear that strike often and without warning. Physical symptoms include chest pain, heart palpitations, shortness of breath, dizziness, abdominal distress, feelings of unreality, and fear of dying.
> ➤ *social phobia:* This causes an overwhelming and disabling fear of scrutiny, embarrassment, or humiliation in social situations that can be so anxiety-producing you may avoid potentially enjoyable activities.
> ➤ *specific phobias:* People with a specific phobia experience extreme, disabling, and irrational fear of something that poses little or no actual danger; the fear leads to avoiding the objects or situations and can cause people to limit their lives unnecessarily.
> ➤ *obsessive-compulsive disorder (OCD):* This problem involves repeated unwanted thoughts or compulsive behaviors that seem impossible to stop or control.

How Much Do You Know about Anxiety Disorders?

1. True or false: Post-traumatic stress disorder (PTSD), once referred to as shell shock or battle fatigue, is a condition that only affects war veterans.

2. True or false: Someone who feels compelled to spend a great deal of time doing things over and over again such as washing his or her hands, checking things, or counting things has an anxiety disorder.

3. What is the most common mental health problem in the United States?
   a) depression
   b) schizophrenia
   c) anxiety disorders

4. Which of the following diseases/disorders are real medical illnesses?
   a) anxiety disorders
   b) diabetes
   c) high blood pressure
   d) all of the above

5. Which of the following are symptoms of an anxiety disorder known as panic disorder?
   a) chest pains or dizziness
   b) nausea or stomach problems
   c) fear of dying
   d) all of the above

6. True or false: Anxiety disorders often occur with other illnesses.

7. True or false: Most people successfully take control of the symptoms of anxiety disorders by sheer willpower and personal strength.

Answers

1. **False.** Anyone who has witnessed a traumatic event is at risk for PTSD. Many people repeatedly relive the trauma in the form of nightmares and disturbing recollections during the day or experience sleep problems, depression, feeling detached or numb, or being easily startled.

2. **True.** A person plagued by the urgent need to engage in certain rituals or who is tormented by unwelcome thoughts may have obsessive-compulsive disorder.

3. **C.** More than 19 million Americans suffer from anxiety disorders.

4. **D.** Anxiety disorders are often related to the biological makeup and experiences of the individual and are often genetic. Anxiety disorders, diabetes, and high blood pressure are all medical illnesses.

5. **D.** All of the above. Panic disorder is characterized by unexpected and repeated episodes of intense fear accompanied by physical symptoms that often mimic symptoms of a heart attack or other life-threatening medical conditions. Left untreated, people with panic disorder can develop so many phobias about places or situations where panic attacks have occurred that they become housebound.

6. **True.** Anxiety disorders often occur with depression, eating disorders, or substance abuse. Anxiety disorders can coexist with illnesses such as heart disease, high blood pressure, irritable bowel syndrome, thyroid conditions, and migraine headaches.

7. **False.** Many people misunderstand anxiety disorders as something that can be overcome by sheer willpower. Wishing the symptoms away does not work, but there are treatments that can help.

Reprinted from "Facts about Anxiety Disorders." National Institute of Mental Health. January 1999. Available online. URL: http://www.nimh.nih.gov/publicat/adfacts.cfm. Accessed December 18, 2006.

Teens can develop any of the recognized anxiety disorders, but some are more common in adolescence than others, and others tend to be age-specific. For example, separation anxiety disorder and specific phobias are more common in younger children between ages six and nine, whereas teens are more likely to experience generalized anxiety disorder, social anxiety disorder, and panic disorder.

Anxiety disorders are among the most common mental, emotional, and behavioral problems in childhood and adolescence. About 13 of every 100 people ages nine to 17 experience some kind of anxiety disorder. Moreover, about half of children and adolescents with anxiety disorders have a second anxiety disorder or other mental or behavioral disorder, such as depression.

WHAT TRIGGERS AN ANXIETY DISORDER?

Stressful things happen in life, such as starting at a new school, moving, or losing a parent in death or divorce. Any of these things can trigger the onset of an anxiety disorder. Some teens, however, develop an anxiety disorder without ever experiencing a specific stressful event.

Children or adolescents are more likely to have an anxiety disorder if either parent has this problem, but doctors don't know whether that's because of heredity, home environment, or a mixture of both. Growing up in a family with a parent who is fearful or anxious can teach you to see the world as a frightening place. If you grow up in a dangerous or uncertain home (perhaps you live in a violent family or community), you may learn to worry or be afraid. Your basic temperament may play a role in some adolescent anxiety disorders, and this also can be a function of genetics, since it's possible to inherit certain temperament characteristics. For example, if you tend to be very shy and quiet in unfamiliar situations, you might be at risk for developing an anxiety disorder.

Sometimes being sick can cause feelings of anxiety. So can abusing alcohol or other drugs. Experimentation with drugs and alcohol during adolescence is common. Some teens who feel anxious try to relax themselves by using alcohol or drugs. They might seem to lessen the anxiety temporarily, but drugs and alcohol create a false sense of security and relaxation that can ultimately make it even harder to function. They're also illegal and can lead to many other problems. Taking drugs or drinking doesn't cure the underlying anxiety problem, and eventually it will only make matters worse. It's easy to overlook the link between what you do today and the consequences that may follow. Some teens feel as if they'll live forever, and that nothing bad will happen to them. They have a false sense of being immune to the problems that others experience, and that can lead them to make poor choices.

Anxiety disorders also may be linked to chemical levels in your brain, which can affect how you feel or act. Your brain has millions of nerve cells called neurons that constantly communicate with each other using chemicals called neurotransmitters. These neurotransmitter messengers are released from one neuron and attach to a receptor on another neuron. If something interferes with this process (maybe a receptor takes in the neurotransmitter too quickly or a neurotransmitter can't attach), it creates an imbalance in the level of neurotransmitters. There are many kinds of neurotransmitters, but two kinds—called serotonin and dopamine—are important in the regulation of your moods. When there's an imbalance of these chemicals, anxiety can occur.

The physical characteristics of your brain also may be linked to the development of certain anxiety disorders. For example, take your body's automatic fight-or-flight reaction discussed earlier in this chapter. If you sense danger (even if it turns out to be a false alarm), your brain alerts a small neural structure called the amygdala, which triggers your fight-or-flight response. Your body responds by boosting your heart rate, quickening your breathing, and activating your sweat glands. But seconds after you get scared, you may realize that there's really no danger after all. You relax, and the fight-or-flight response screeches to a halt. But your amygdala is programmed to remember whatever it was that set the whole process in motion in case it happens again. This is how your brain protects you from future danger. The next time you encounter the same thing that scared you—even if it's really harmless—your amygdala may activate the same anxiety reaction. In some people the amygdala overreacts, which can lead to an anxiety disorder.

No matter what the cause, teens with untreated anxiety disorders are at higher risk to perform poorly in school and to have less developed social skills; as discussed earlier, they are also more vulnerable to substance abuse.

TREATMENT

Anxiety disorders are typically treated in two ways: with psychotherapy and, for some conditions, medications. Both approaches can be effective for most disorders, but whether the treatment includes therapy or drugs depends on you, your doctor, and the particular anxiety disorder you have. For example, only psychotherapy has been found to be effective for specific phobias. Because medications in addition to talk therapy may be effective in many other types of anxiety disorders, when you look for a therapist you should find out whether and how any medications will be prescribed.

Talk therapy: the best choice. Sitting down and talking to a psychotherapist about your worries is often the best way to treat anxiety disorders. This kind of support can be enormously helpful as you sort through your problems.

Two types of psychotherapy have proved effective in treating anxiety disorders: behavioral therapy and cognitive therapy. *Behavioral therapy* focuses on changing a person's specific actions using a variety of ways to stop unwanted behaviors and learning new ones. *Cognitive therapy* teaches you how to understand and change the way you actually think about things, so you can react differently in the future to the situations that make you anxious. These two treatments help you play an active role in unlearning some of your fear, while you learn new ways to think and act when confronted with anxiety. You'll learn how to manage stress so it doesn't spiral out of control. You'll also learn how to figure out the times when you're feeling anxious, how to measure your anxiety, and how to recognize what triggers those feelings. Then you will practice ways to reduce it. And that's not all. You'll learn what worsens your fear and what eases it. Techniques may include relaxation and breathing exercises, along with exposure therapy, in which you're exposed to whatever it is that's triggering your anxiety. If it's done with proper support and new coping skills, exposure can help reduce even intense fear—such as fear of flying, fear of crowds, or fear of snakes or dogs.

Medications. A number of medications that were originally approved to treat depression are also effective for anxiety disorders. This includes the newest antidepressants, called selective serotonin reuptake inhibitors (SSRIs). The SSRIs work for both depression and anxiety because both conditions involve an imbalance of the neurotransmitter serotonin. SSRI medications help restore the normal balance of serotonin and therefore can improve both depression and anxiety. Other antianxiety medications include groups of drugs called benzodiazepines and beta-blockers. Of course, most teens with an anxiety disorder don't need medication, but for people with severe problems, the right medication can help to reduce symptoms.

It should be noted that the U.S. Food and Drug Administration requires a warning when SSRIs are prescribed to teens, because some adolescents have experienced serious side effects (including suicide attempts or suicidal thoughts) shortly after beginning to take these medications. Still, most experts believe that SSRIs are helpful to most teens who are prescribed these drugs.

If your doctor has prescribed medication to help treat an anxiety disorder, you'll most likely be started with a very small dose, which is gradually increased until the best dosage for you is reached. It may take several weeks or more to get the dosage just right. You may find that one drug doesn't work at all, and your doctor might switch you to a different medication two or three times until you find the right one. It's very important to understand that if one medication doesn't work, your doctor should try another until he or she determines the right one or the right combination. As with any medication, it's very important to take these medications exactly as prescribed and to tell your doctor about any side effects.

ARE YOU ANXIOUS?

Some people just naturally worry more than others. Do you think of every single way things could go wrong? Here's a list of common worries you might experience in a typical day:

> ▶ "What if I miss the bus?"
> ▶ "Are my friends going to drop me?"
> ▶ "Is my girlfriend going to break up with me?"
> ▶ "How will I get to play practice if my mom is sick?"
> ▶ "Why don't any boys like me?"
> ▶ "Will I have enough money to buy lunch today?"
> ▶ "What if my teacher gives me an F after I studied all night?"
> ▶ "Will I make the team?"
> ▶ "Will I play well enough to stay on the team?"

Do any of those sound familiar? Occasional worries are normal, but if these kinds of concerns preoccupy your thoughts, they may eventually become a regular part of the way you live each day, and they'll tend to sustain your anxiety. In fact, experts believe that anxious people tend to automatically think in ways that keep anxiety going.

Now that you've learned a bit about anxiety in general and how it's different from instinctual fear, you may have a better idea whether you might be worrying too much. The good news is that anxiety can be treated, so if your worries get too overwhelming and start interfering with your life, something needs to be done. The next step to take if you think you might have a problem is to find someone to talk with about your worries.

WHAT YOU NEED TO KNOW

▶ Anxiety disorders affect as many as one of every eight teens of every age, color, religion, and economic status and are more common among girls.

▶ *Instinctual fear* is a reaction to an actual danger signal that involves physical and mental tension so you can protect yourself; once the danger has passed, the fear goes away.

Common Anxiety Pitfalls

It's a catastrophe! No matter what's happening, you come up with the most extreme negative consequence imaginable and assume it's going to happen. You'll be the *only* girl in your school who doesn't have a date for the semiformal. You're the *stupidest* guy in your entire class because you failed an English test. You *know* you'll make a mistake during your speech and humiliate yourself in front of the entire student body because you're the *worst* public speaker in the history of the school.

Jumping to conclusions. At the first sign of a problem, you immediately jump to conclusions. Feeling a knot in your stomach before a test means you have stomach cancer. The principal calling your name means you're being expelled, even though you haven't done anything wrong. That bruise that suddenly appears on your thigh means you have leukemia.

It's inevitable! Because something unpleasant happened once, you automatically assume it will happen again. For example, since you got nervous right before the last math test, you figure you're doomed to anxiety before every single math test.

I'm next! Whatever happens nearby could personally affect you, and you'll probably experience it next. For example, if there's a burglary across town, you assume you'll be next to get mugged.

It could happen! You focus on one part of an issue that could create a problem and ignore the nonthreatening parts. For example, you worry that you could forget how to solve one type of geometry problem although you've studied hard for the whole test and you've gotten almost all of the problems right during practice tests.

- The physical and mental tension of *anxiety* is similar to fear except there isn't usually any actual danger to trigger the feeling. The feeling comes from the *anticipation* of future danger.
- Each anxiety disorder has unique features, but they all involve excessive fear and dread without clear danger.
- There are six types of anxiety disorders: *generalized anxiety disorder, panic disorder, post-traumatic stress disorder, obsessive-compulsive disorder, social phobias,* and *specific phobias.*
- Separation anxiety disorder and specific phobias are more common in younger kids between ages six and nine; teens are more likely to experience generalized anxiety disorder, social anxiety disorder, and panic disorder.
- Anxiety disorders are among the most common mental, emotional, and behavioral problems in childhood and adolescence.
- About half of teens with anxiety disorders have a second anxiety disorder or other mental or behavioral disorder, such as depression.
- Stress (starting at a new school, moving, or losing a parent in death or divorce) can trigger the onset of an anxiety disorder, but some teens develop an anxiety disorder without ever experiencing a specific stressful event.
- Children or adolescents are more likely to have an anxiety disorder if either parent has this problem.
- Anxiety disorders may be linked to chemical levels in your brain.
- Untreated anxiety disorders are linked to poor school performance, social skills problems, and substance abuse.
- Anxiety disorders are typically treated with psychotherapy and, for some conditions, medications.
- Behavioral therapy and cognitive therapy are effective in treating anxiety disorders.
- *Behavioral therapy* changes a person's specific actions using a variety of ways to stop unwanted behavior and learn new ones; *cognitive therapy* teaches you how to understand and change the way you think about things, so you can react differently in the future to the situations that make you anxious.

2

Getting an Evaluation: Where to Turn

Sarah struggled with overwhelming feelings of anxiety for several months before she finally broke down and shared her feelings with a friend. "Some mornings I'm just so freaked out I can't even go to school," the 15-year-old confessed. "I feel so much pressure. My parents are always fighting at home. I worry about grades, and I get so tense before a test that I can't remember anything." In fact, Sarah's anxiety had reached such high levels that she could barely function at school or at home, where she would shut herself away, binging on junk food in an effort to soothe her feelings.

"I feel like everything is closing in on me," she told her best friend, "and sometimes I worry that I might do something to make all of this just go away."

Alarmed, Sarah's friend encouraged her to talk to their favorite science teacher, who convinced her to visit the school's counselor. After a session with Sarah, the counselor called her parents and gave them a referral to a psychologist trained in handling anxiety disorders. After several months of intense psychotherapy, Sarah reports that she is feeling far more in control of her emotions and that she's managing her anxiety.

If you've been struggling with anxious feelings like Sarah was, you're probably quite aware that there's something wrong. Of course, everyone feels anxious sometimes, but if your problems are persistent and interfere with the way you'd like to live your life, you need to check with a health care professional to find out if it's a problem that needs to be treated.

MAKING THE DECISION TO GET HELP

Although psychotherapy is extremely helpful for a wide variety of mental health problems, you'd be amazed at the number of people who are still reluctant to seek this kind of help. If you had a toothache, would you avoid going to the dentist? If you broke your ankle, would you resist a visit to the emergency room to have it set in a cast? Would you think it seemed weak to have a flu shot to prevent the flu? Of course not! Yet many people balk at seeking mental health care, as if needing help for a mental problem were some sort of embarrassing weakness. It's not!

Still, making the decision to seek help for a problem can be hard. If you're thinking about getting help, you should be proud of yourself.

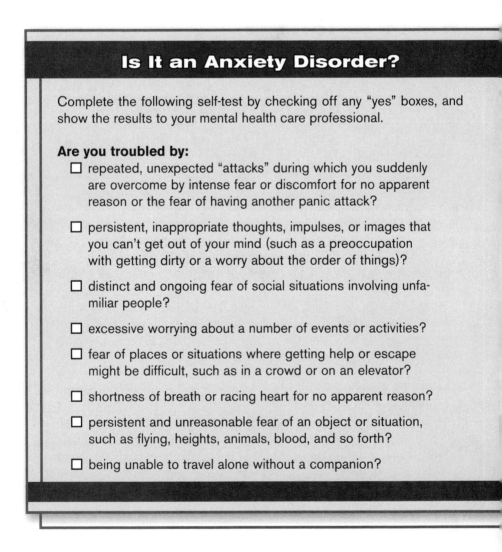

Is It an Anxiety Disorder?

Complete the following self-test by checking off any "yes" boxes, and show the results to your mental health care professional.

Are you troubled by:

☐ repeated, unexpected "attacks" during which you suddenly are overcome by intense fear or discomfort for no apparent reason or the fear of having another panic attack?

☐ persistent, inappropriate thoughts, impulses, or images that you can't get out of your mind (such as a preoccupation with getting dirty or a worry about the order of things)?

☐ distinct and ongoing fear of social situations involving unfamiliar people?

☐ excessive worrying about a number of events or activities?

☐ fear of places or situations where getting help or escape might be difficult, such as in a crowd or on an elevator?

☐ shortness of breath or racing heart for no apparent reason?

☐ persistent and unreasonable fear of an object or situation, such as flying, heights, animals, blood, and so forth?

☐ being unable to travel alone without a companion?

Knowing that you've got a problem and wanting to get help means you're taking responsibility for yourself.

It may be your idea to go to therapy because of a problem you're having, or maybe your parents or a teacher suggested it because they noticed that you're having trouble with anxious feelings. Some teens in this situation feel relieved that someone is helping them, but others might feel that their behavior is being criticized. If therapy is someone else's idea, you may feel like resisting the whole thing. If this is the case, try telling yourself that you'll give it a week or two just to see how it goes. You'll probably be surprised at how good it feels to talk to somebody about what's bothering you.

☐ spending too much time each day doing things over and over again (for example, hand washing, checking things, or counting)?

More days than not, do you
☐ feel restless?

☐ feel easily fatigued or distracted?

☐ experience muscle tension or problems sleeping?

More days than not, are you
☐ sad or depressed?

☐ uninterested in life?

☐ feeling worthless or guilty?

☐ experiencing changes in sleeping or eating habits?

☐ reliving a traumatic event through thoughts, games, distressing dreams, or flashbacks?

☐ finding that your anxiety interferes with your daily life?

Reprinted with permission by the Anxiety Disorders Association of America.

You might worry about what your classmates will say or think if they find out you're seeing a therapist. First of all, the only way kids will know is if you tell. Second, you may be surprised to find out how many kids in your class have seen a therapist already. When you visit the therapist, he or she will spend some time talking, listening, and observing to better evaluate your problems. This is how the therapist can help you figure out the problem and how to improve things. It might take you a couple of sessions before you feel comfortable sharing openly. That's perfectly okay; it takes time to build trust, and trust is the most important ingredient in therapy. You've got to trust the person if you're going to be honest when you talk about personal things such as feelings, hopes, dreams, ideas, relationships, problems, and disappointments. A therapist has plenty of training and experience in how to listen to you and allow you to take your time talking about your situation.

Finding a therapist can take time. You may not be sure of the best place to go for help. Some kids feel comfortable talking about their anxiety to their parents. Other kids turn to a teacher they trust, or they might confide in their school's counselor, psychologist, or nurse. The important thing is to talk to someone you trust about your feelings and fears, someone who can offer you guidance about taking the next step to get help. Alternatively, you seek advice from someone you trust who has experience in mental health, such as a doctor, nurse, social worker, or religious counselor. Your family doctor can help determine if your symptoms are caused by an anxiety disorder, a medical condition, or both.

If your doctor or school counselor thinks that you might have a serious problem with anxiety, the next step is to get a referral to a psychologist, a psychiatrist, a social worker, or a pastoral counselor.

FINDING A MENTAL HEALTH EXPERT ON YOUR OWN

If you prefer not to involve your doctor or anyone at school, you or your parents can look for a mental health expert on your own. There are three questions to ask when searching for a mental health professional:

➤ How much expertise does he or she have with cognitive-behavioral techniques?
➤ How much experience does he or she have in treating anxiety disorders?
➤ How comfortable do you feel with this person?

The easiest way to find a highly trained cognitive-behavioral therapist is to visit the Web site for the Academy of Cognitive Therapy (http://www.academyofct.org) or the Association for Behavioral and Cognitive Therapies (http://www.aabt.org). Both groups are multidisciplinary, professional organizations that promote the research and practice of cognitive and behavioral therapies. The Academy of

Who Can Provide Referrals for Treatment

If you have access to the Internet, the government offers a Mental Health Services Locator at http://www.mentalhealth.samhsa.gov/databases. This Web site provides information about mental health services and resources in your state. You can access this information by clicking on your state, which will reveal a list of helpful resources and referrals. Other sources for referrals include

➤ family doctors

➤ psychiatrists, psychologists, social workers, and mental health counselors

➤ religious leaders or counselors

➤ health maintenance organizations

➤ community mental health centers

➤ hospital psychiatry departments and outpatient clinics

➤ university- or medical school–affiliated programs

➤ state hospital outpatient clinics

➤ social service agencies

➤ private clinics and facilities

➤ schools

➤ employee assistance programs

➤ student assistance programs

Cognitive Therapy is the only organization of this type that certifies therapists through an objective skills–based evaluation process. You can find a list of certified therapists on their Web site.

If you don't live near a certified cognitive therapist, you can try any of the following methods for identifying a therapist who may help you:

> ▸ If you live near a university, its department of psychiatry or psychology may offer private and/or sliding scale–fee clinic treatment options.
> ▸ Check the Yellow Pages under "mental health," "health," "social services," "suicide prevention," "crisis intervention services," "hotlines," "hospitals," or "physicians" for phone numbers and addresses.
> ▸ Call your local medical or mental health societies for referrals.
> ▸ Call national professional societies such as the American Psychiatric Association, the American Psychological Association, the National Association of Social Workers, or the American Association of Pastoral Counselors for names of their members near you.
> ▸ If you feel that you're in crisis, the emergency room doctor or a crisis intervention counselor at your local hospital may be able to give you temporary help for a mental health problem; he or she will also be able to tell you where and how to get further help.

WHAT KIND OF SPECIALIST?

You may be referred to different types of specialists trained to treat anxiety disorders. How do you tell the difference among psychologists, psychiatrists, social workers, and pastoral counselors?

It's best to get treatment from a professional who has specialized training in the types of treatments that work best for anxiety problems: cognitive-behavioral therapy and/or behavioral therapy. Since medication also may be used to help treat anxiety disorders, the psychologist, social worker, or counselor will probably work closely with a psychiatrist or other physician who can prescribe medications if needed. (If you live in New Mexico or Louisiana, specially trained medical psychologists in those states can prescribe medication to you directly.) The following is a general breakdown of the different experts to whom you might be referred.

Psychologist. This mental health expert specializes in the diagnosis and treatment of a person's mental or emotional problems. Clinical psychologists often use a range of tests to assess, diagnose, and treat patients. A psychologist usually holds a doctoral degree (Ph.D., Psy.D., or Ed.D.) from a university or professional school, with four or more years of graduate school and a year of supervised internship. Most states also require an additional year of supervised experience for a professional license in this area. (In a few states, professionals with master's degrees in psychology can be licensed as psychologists.)

There are many types of psychologists, including clinical psychologists, counseling psychologists, developmental psychologists, and school psychologists.

A clinical psychologist is the most common type of psychologist in a treatment setting; these experts have Ph.D.'s and can assess and treat mental, emotional, and behavioral disorders. This type of mental health expert helps people deal with all kinds of mental health issues. They handle both temporary problems caused by stressful situations and more severe, chronic conditions, including anxiety disorders. You'll find them working in private practice, in hospitals, and in clinics. Because they are not medical doctors, clinical psychologists in most states can't prescribe medication. Some specialize in certain types of problems, while others specialize in certain groups, such as children or adolescents.

A counseling psychologist has a Ph.D. and helps people cope with everyday life. Counseling psychologists help people recognize their own strengths and resources for coping with their problems and teaches them how to use their strengths to their advantage in all situations, including school and personal relationships. They advise patients based on various test results and interviews and often work in university counseling centers, hospitals, and private practice. Developmental psychologists specialize in behavior and development during specific stages of life, such as childhood or adolescence. A school psychologist often has a master's degree and works with teachers, parents, and administrators to solve learning and behavioral problems and help teachers with classroom management strategies.

A psychologist studies and understands emotions and behavior processes from a scientific angle and applies this knowledge to help teens understand and change their behavior. Many psychologists have received specialty training, such as in family psychotherapy, anxiety disorders, or neuropsychology. Because psychology is such a broad field, it's important for you to find out if the psychologist you're considering has good training and experience in the particular kinds of problems that concern you.

Psychologists who care for patients must meet certification and licensing requirements in the state in which they practice. Requirements include training, experience, an approved internship, and examinations. There are various boards that accredit qualifying psychologists, including the American Psychological Association and the American Board of Professional Psychology.

Psychiatrist. A psychiatrist is a medical doctor (either an M.D. or a D.O.) who specializes in the diagnosis and treatment of disorders of thinking, feeling, or behavior. Psychiatrists can prescribe medication and therefore often work with psychologists in prescribing antidepressants or other drug treatments.

Psychiatrists must complete four years of medical school and at least three years of residency training in medicine, neurology, and general psychiatry. After completing medical school, graduates must pass a licensing test given by the board of medical examiners for the state in which they want to work. Psychiatrists must then take and pass the certifying examination given by the Board of Psychiatry and Neurology. A psychiatrist also can be board certified in child and adolescent psychiatry with extra years of training. Psychiatrists must pass a written examination that covers the basic sciences, psychiatry, and psychiatric subspecialties, along with an oral exam to assess clinical skills. Psychiatrists must be recertified every 10 years.

Social worker. A clinical social worker provides mental health services to prevent, diagnose, and treat mental, behavioral, and emotional disorders. Clinical social workers must have a master's or doctorate degree in social work, with an emphasis on clinical experience. They must undergo a supervised clinical field internship and have at least two years of postgraduate supervised clinical social work. They may be licensed by their state after successfully passing an exam and meeting all requirements. All states have licensing, certification, or registration requirements regarding social work practice and the use of professional titles. Social workers with a master's degree in social work (MSW) may be eligible for the Academy of Certified Social Workers (ACSW), the qualified clinical social worker (QCSW), or the diplomate in clinical social work (DCSW) credential based on their professional experience.

Licensed professional counselor. A licensed professional counselor (LPC) applies mental health, psychological, and human development principles through cognitive, affective, behavioral, or systematic intervention strategies that address wellness, personal growth, or career development, as well as pathology. LPCs work in a variety of settings including schools, mental health centers, public service agencies, and health care systems. To become an LPC, one must obtain at least a master's degree in counseling or a related discipline, successfully pass the National Counselor Exam (NCE), and receive two years of supervision prior to receiving a license to practice counseling.

Pastoral counselor. A pastoral counselor is trained in both psychology and theology. You should consider meeting with a pastoral counselor if you wish to address your anxieties in the context of religion and spirituality. In general, the fees of pastoral counselors are lower than those of other health care professionals; counseling by a certified pastoral counselor is generally covered by health care plans only if the pastoral counselor is licensed by the state. Pastoral counselors are not medical doctors and may not prescribe medication. While many pastoral counselors are licensed by the state, most states do not require it. However, laws vary significantly from state to state.

When you're looking for just the right professional, assess how well the person helps you understand your problem and the treatment and how comfortable you feel during your session. Don't be afraid to spend some time checking out different experts at first, before you decide with whom you'll want to begin treatment. And don't give up if you don't happen to find a good match right away. Keep up the search, because eventually you'll be glad you did.

Psychotherapist. This term is a general catchall for just about anyone who counsels clients. A psychotherapist could be a clinical psychologist, psychiatrist, registered psychiatric nurse, clinical social worker, marriage therapist, or family therapist. Drug and alcohol counselors, ordained priests, ministers, and rabbis may practice psychotherapy without a license. In some states, a person with a master's degree in education or psychology may also practice psychotherapy without a license.

ONCE YOU'VE FOUND AN EXPERT

Once you have your referral to a mental health specialist, your parents have probably talked to this person on the phone, discussed payment options and insurance issues, and arranged for your first appointment. On this first visit, try to get a feel for whether you're comfortable working with this individual. This is the time to ask questions, and some you might want to ask include the following:

☐ What is your approach to treatment?
☐ How much experience do you have treating anxiety disorders?

☐ Can you prescribe medication or refer me to someone who can, if that's necessary?

☐ How long might treatment take?

☐ How often will we need to meet?

☐ Will my family be included in therapy?

You'll work with this mental health professional as a team to discover the exact nature of your anxiety. At the beginning, therapy sessions are focused on discussing what you'd like to work on and setting goals. Together, you'll develop a plan to treat your anxiety disorder that may involve medications, cognitive-behavioral or other talk therapy, or a combination of methods. That's why it's so important that you feel comfortable working with this person and that you feel confident that you can ask questions about the process. It's also important that you feel comfortable with whatever therapy the mental health professional suggests. The more you trust this person and feel comfortable in exploring your feelings, the better.

During the first visit, your therapist will probably ask you to talk a bit about yourself and what problems, concerns, and symptoms you're having. Before treatment can start, the therapist must complete a careful evaluation to figure out whether your symptoms are caused by an anxiety disorder and, if so, which anxiety disorder you have. The therapist also will try to figure out if you have any other mental health issues going on at the same time—which is not unusual. If a client has a drug or alcohol problem or some other condition that may affect the anxiety disorder, those conditions will have to be treated too.

Because all anxiety disorders aren't treated in the same way, it's important to figure out exactly what your problems are before deciding on the type of treatment. If you've been treated in the past for an anxiety disorder by a different therapist, you should be ready to tell the therapist what treatment you tried. Don't be embarrassed at having seen other experts before or of not finishing treatment with that person. Your current therapist will want to know if you've taken any type of medication before for your symptoms; if you have, be sure to bring the list with you, along with the dosage. How did you take the medication, and for how long? If you had psychotherapy, the therapist will want to know what kind (cognitive, behavioral, or both) and how often you went for treatment.

After one or two sessions, you can expect the therapist to explain what he or she thinks about your situation, how therapy could help, and what the process will involve. Together, you and your therapist will decide on what your goals will be and whether you'll meet once a week, every other week, or once a month. Once your therapist

What Do All Those Initials Mean?

Mental health professionals may have initials after their names to indicate a variety of credentials. Here's a chart to decode the meanings:

AAMFT	American Association for Marriage and Family Therapy (cert)*
AAPH	American Association of Professional Hypnotherapists (cert)
ABFamP	American Board of Family Psychology (cert)
ABMP	American Board of Medical Psychotherapy (cert)
ABPH	American Board of Psychological Hypnosis
ABPP	American Board of Professional Psychology
ACP	advanced clinical practitioner (lic)**
ACSW	Academy of Clinical Social Workers (cert)
ACT	Academy of Cognitive Therapy (cert)
BCCS	board certified in clinical social work (cert)
BCDSW	board certified diplomate in clinical social work (cert)
CCAP	board certified in child and adolescent psychology (cert)
CCMHC	certified clinical mental health counselor (cert)
CCSW	certified clinical social worker (lic)
CISW	certified independent social worker (cert)
CMFT	certified marriage and family therapist (cert)
CP	certified psychologist (lic); clinical psychologist (lic)
CSW	certified social worker (lic); clinical social worker (lic)
D/AABM	diplomate, American Academy of Behavioral Medicine (cert)
D/ABPN	diplomate, American Board of Psychiatry and Neurology
DSW	doctor of social work
Ed.D.	doctor of education
LCP	licensed clinical psychologist (lic)
LCSW	licensed clinical social worker (lic)
LGSW	licensed graduate social worker (lic)

(continues)

(continued)

LICSW	licensed independent clinical social worker (lic)
LMFC	licensed marriage and family counselor (lic)
LMFCC	licensed marriage, family, and child counselor (lic)
LMFT	licensed marriage and family therapist (lic)
LMHC	licensed mental health counselor (lic)
LP	licensed psychologist (lic)
LPA	licensed psychological associate (lic)
LPC	licensed professional counselor (lic)
LSP	licensed school psychologist (lic)
LSW	licensed social worker (lic)
MC	master of counseling
MFC	marriage and family counselor (lic)
MFCC	marriage, family, and child counselor (lic)
MFCT	marriage, family, and child therapist (lic)
MSS	master of social science
MSSW	master of science in social work
MSW	master of social work
NAMHC	National Academy of Mental Health Counselors (cert)
NBCC	National Board of Certified Counselors (cert)
NCC	National Certified Counselor (cert)
NRHSPP	National Register of Health Services Providers in Psychology (cert)
Ph.D.	doctor of philosophy
Psy.D.	doctor of psychology
RHCP	registered health care provider (cert)
RISW	registered independent social worker (lic)
Sc.D.	doctor of science (lic)
SW	social worker (lic)

*Indicates that the person is certified by the group or other agency.
**Indicates that the person is licensed by the state or other agency.

understands exactly what's going on in your life, he or she might teach you new skills or help you think about a situation in a new way. Your therapist might teach you how to brush up on your friend-building skills or your coping skills, helping you build confidence, express yourself, or manage your angry feelings. If you have specific fears, you'll work on those. Most anxiety disorders can be treated within a relatively short time. Sticking to your treatment schedule and keeping your appointments will help you feel better much more quickly.

A WORD ABOUT PRIVACY

Janine came to school one day in tears. During study hall Janine confessed to her best friend, Debbie, that she was failing two courses at school and was so depressed she didn't think she could keep coming to school. Knowing that Janine had been seeing a therapist, Debbie asked her whether she had told the therapist about her feelings. "I can't," Janine said. "I'm afraid the therapist will tell my parents."

If you're like most kids, one of the issues you're going to be worried about is exactly how private your psychotherapy experience will be. Most kids worry whether the therapist will tell their parents or teachers what they confide during sessions. Since home and school are often areas where kids have problems, it's not surprising that

---

If You're Thinking of Harming Yourself...

Tell someone who can help right away or

- ▸ Call your doctor's office.
- ▸ Call 911 for emergency services.
- ▸ Go to the nearest hospital emergency room.
- ▸ Call your local crisis intervention program.
- ▸ Call the toll-free, 24-hour hotline of the National Suicide Prevention Lifeline at (800) 273-TALK (800-273-8255) to be connected to a trained counselor at a suicide crisis center nearest you.

you'll wonder whether you can trust the therapist to keep any of your criticisms or revelations private.

You should know that therapists respect the privacy of their clients, and they keep things they're told confidential. In fact, it's against the law for a therapist to reveal what a client says during treatment. You can feel confident that your therapist won't tell anyone else what you discuss in your sessions, unless you give your permission. It is important for you, your parents, and your therapist to discuss what will be kept private and what will be shared with your parents. The only exception is if your therapist believes that you may harm yourself or others or if you inform your therapist that someone is harming you.

At the beginning of treatment, your parents may be asked to provide information about your family's medical history, your home environment, your physical and emotional development, and your friendships. Your parents also will be included in the discussion of the assessment and a treatment plan. The therapist may also discuss with your parents what their role will be during treatment (if any), how they should communicate with him or her, a schedule for feedback and updates, and how to coordinate with outside resources or professionals.

If you're worried whether what you tell the therapist will stay private, you must discuss this during your first meeting. Ask the therapist for his or her feelings about confidentiality and what he or she would or wouldn't confide to your parents. It's important to feel comfortable with your therapist so you can talk openly about your situation.

IF IT DOESN'T WORK OUT

Not every dating relationship works out, so you shouldn't be surprised to hear that not every match between therapist and client is successful either. Sometimes, you and the therapist may just not seem to have a good fit. It doesn't mean the therapist isn't any good, and it doesn't mean that there's anything wrong with you. Sometimes two people just don't hit it off or seem to connect very well. The earlier you figure this out, the better, because there's no sense in struggling along in a therapeutic relationship that doesn't feel helpful.

If you don't feel comfortable with this expert, you're certainly within your rights to seek help elsewhere. Sometimes a person might need to visit several therapists before finding someone who clicks, and that's perfectly okay. You might worry that the therapist may be hurt or disappointed if you want to find a different professional, but remember—you're paying a therapist to help you. If you don't feel comfortable with the person, it's going to be very hard to get better, and getting better is what this experience is all about.

Keep in mind, however, that if the expert has prescribed medication for you, it's important not to discontinue it abruptly. Certain drugs must be tapered off under the supervision of your physician.

WHAT YOU NEED TO KNOW

▸ If your mother or father, teacher, school counselor, or family doctor thinks that you might have a problem with anxiety, the next step is to get a referral to a psychologist, a psychiatrist, a social worker, or a pastoral counselor.

▸ A psychologist is a mental health expert (usually with a Ph.D.) who specializes in the diagnosis and treatment of a person's mental or emotional problems.

▸ A psychiatrist is a medical doctor (either an M.D. or a D.O.) who can prescribe medication and who specializes in the diagnosis and treatment of disorders of thinking, feeling, or behavior.

▸ A clinical social worker provides mental health services to prevent, diagnose, and treat mental, behavioral, and emotional disorders.

▸ A pastoral counselor is trained in both psychology and theology.

▸ *Psychotherapist* is a general term that could refer to a clinical psychologist, psychiatrist, registered psychiatric nurse, clinical social worker, marriage therapist, or family therapist.

▸ Therapy sessions first focus on setting goals and developing a plan to treat an anxiety disorder that may involve medications, cognitive-behavioral or other talk therapy, or a combination of methods.

▸ It's against the law for a therapist to reveal what a client says during treatment, so your therapist won't tell anyone (including your parents) what you discuss in your sessions, unless you give your permission. The only exception is if your therapist believes that you may harm yourself or others or if your therapist has reason to believe that someone is harming you.

▸ If you don't feel comfortable with your therapist, you can and should seek help from a different therapist.

3

Treatment: Therapy and Pills

When Terry was diagnosed with obsessive-compulsive disorder, he felt completely different from everyone else. It seemed to him that he was walking around with a big "OC" sign on his forehead, as if everyone in school knew about it. Terry was embarrassed and sometimes felt as if he was the only person who suffered from this problem. When Terry looked around his class, all he saw were laughing, happy, well-adjusted teens. He didn't realize that several of his classmates were hiding very similar issues behind such cheerful masks.

If you've been diagnosed with an anxiety disorder, you may feel like Terry, but the important thing is to understand that anxiety disorders are common and can be treated. You're not doomed to live with constant worries. Because an anxiety disorder is a real emotional disturbance and not a moral failing, it can be treated so that you can go on to have a healthy and full life.

Try not to be discouraged if some of your friends or family misunderstand your problem. Many people who don't understand anxiety disorders may think you should be able to overcome these anxious symptoms by sheer willpower. But as you know, anxiety disorders can't be wished away. If they could, you would have wished them away long ago. You can't snap out of it just by wanting to.

Of course, just because it's possible to treat anxiety disorders doesn't mean it's going to be easy. It can be a challenge to find the right treatment, and it will involve lots of hard work on your part. But anxiety disorders and phobias are highly treatable with some combination of talk therapy (psychotherapy) and medication.

Both approaches can be effective for most disorders. The choice of using one or the other or both depends on the patient's and the doctor's preference and on the guidelines for the particular anxiety disorder you have. For instance, psychotherapy alone has been found effective for specific phobias.

Yet for some reason, only about a third of people who have an anxiety disorder are ever treated. This is unfortunate, since there is no reason to suffer from so much anxiety in your life.

Before treatment can begin, your doctor must conduct a careful diagnostic evaluation to determine that your symptoms are due to an anxiety disorder, which anxiety disorders you may have, and what other conditions or issues you may have at the same time. Because anxiety disorders aren't all treated the same, it's important to figure out exactly what's going on in your life before starting a course of treatment. For example, depression or drug use has a big impact on your life, so it's necessary to treat that problem along with the anxiety disorder.

If you've been treated before for an anxiety disorder, tell the doctor what treatments you've already tried. If it was a medication, what was the dosage, was it gradually increased, and how long did you take it? If you had psychotherapy, what kind was it, and how often did you attend sessions? Often someone might think a treatment has failed, when really the person just didn't hang in there long enough to see if it would work, or he or she didn't receive the best treatment indicated for their condition.

When you undergo treatment for an anxiety disorder, keep in mind that you and your doctor or therapist will be working together as a team. Together, you're trying to find the approach that works best for you. If one treatment doesn't work, the odds are that another one will. At the same time, newer, even better treatments are continually being developed in research labs around the country, so don't give up hope.

COEXISTING CONDITIONS

If you've got one anxiety disorder, it's not unusual to also have another type of anxiety disorder or a different mental health problem as well. For example, many teens with panic disorder or social phobia also experience depression. Teens often have an eating disorder or substance abuse problem along with their anxiety disorder. These problems must be treated as well, ideally at the same time as the anxiety disorder.

However, if you're having trouble with drugs or alcohol in addition to your anxiety disorder, most experts agree that you should get treatment for your chemical dependency first. Consider participating in a long-term recovery program such as Alcoholics Anonymous (AA) or Narcotics Anonymous (NA). Once you conquer your drug or alcohol dependency, you'll have a much better chance of recovering from anxiety.

It's also very important that you tell your doctor that you have a past or current problem with drug abuse. That will help your doctor figure out which of your symptoms are related directly to anxiety and choose the right medication for you. For instance, antidepressants (which are also used to treat anxiety) or buspirone are usually better choices for anxious patients who have a substance abuse problem, because these drugs don't lead to dependency or abuse.

IF YOUR ANXIETY COMES BACK

If you've recovered from an anxiety disorder and it comes back over time, don't consider yourself a treatment failure. Recurrences can be treated just as effectively as the first episode. In fact, the skills you learned in dealing with your problem the first time can help you cope even more quickly with a setback.

PSYCHOTHERAPY

Psychotherapy doesn't mean you'll be lying on a couch analyzing your dreams. Modern psychotherapy for anxiety disorders is usually aimed at either changing your behavior (behavioral therapy) or changing your thoughts and your behavior (cognitive-behavioral therapy). If you're being treated with this type of therapy, you'll meet each week for about 12 weeks with a trained mental health professional (a psychiatrist, psychologist, social worker, or counselor) to learn how to deal with your anxiety symptoms.

The aim of both CBT and behavioral therapy is to ease your anxiety by eliminating your beliefs or behaviors that reinforce your anxiety disorder. For example, if you're afraid of dogs and you keep avoiding dogs, you'll never learn that they're harmless. If you hate speaking in public and avoid any opportunity to give a speech, you'll never learn you can survive the experience. Similarly, if you have OCD, the compulsive rituals you perform probably ease your anxiety and prevent you from testing a hypothesis about danger or contamination. Ultimately, to overcome a specific phobia, you must come face-to-face with the thing that triggers your anxiety. To be effective, CBT or behavioral therapy must be directed at your specific anxieties. Therefore, a treatment plan that works well for somebody with a specific phobia about dogs isn't going to help a person with OCD who keeps thinking about killing his father.

Sometimes this type of therapy is conducted in a group setting of teens with similar problems. Group therapy works particularly well for teens with social phobia.

Moreover, once you've successfully treated your anxiety disorder with CBT, it usually is gone for good. There is some evidence that for people with panic disorder, the beneficial effects of CBT last longer than the effects of medications. The same may be true for OCD, PTSD, and social phobia.

You won't have to worry about any side effects of CBT or behavioral therapy beyond the temporary discomfort of increased anxiety. Your therapist should be well trained in the various treatment techniques.

COGNITIVE-BEHAVIORAL THERAPY (CBT)

Research has shown that CBT works very well for several types of anxiety disorders—particularly panic disorder and social phobia. This form of therapy focuses on healing unhelpful thought patterns, but it's much more than just positive thinking. Take five minutes and monitor the thoughts that pop into your head in any given day, and you'll be surprised at the constant flow of "chatter" that goes on. When these thoughts are constantly negative, they can disrupt your life and very subtly influence your outlook so that the glass is always half empty, not half full. Teens with anxiety problems frequently tell themselves they won't be able to deal with the situation they fear. When Brittany got her math paper back marked with a big red C, her automatic thought kicked in: "Another C. I'll never understand math. I'm the worst math student in my class, and no matter how hard I study, I'll never get an A. I'm just dumb in math." A thought pattern like this can carry great emotional weight without ever providing helpful answers. Brittany probably never even realized how damaging such a string of negative self-talk could be.

Automatic thoughts are always there, and we don't pay attention to most of them, which is fine. But in situations where you're having problems, it's in your interest to find out what automatic thoughts you're having, no matter what the problem might be—social phobia, PTSD, obsessive-compulsive disorder, and so on. Whenever you're confronted with a situation or object that increases your anxiety, it's to your benefit to focus on your automatic thought behind the anxiety.

Cognition. The cognitive part of cognitive-behavioral therapy focuses on first identifying and then changing the problem thinking patterns or automatic thoughts that have kept you from overcoming your fears. The first step to addressing an anxiety disorder is to become aware of the thoughts and feelings behind it. Checking out exactly what your automatic thoughts are can help you resolve your problems.

For example, someone with panic disorder undergoing CBT might come to see that his panic attacks aren't really heart attacks as he had feared. Or a person with obsessive-compulsive disorder might be guided into realizing that her hands aren't really contaminated with deadly germs requiring disinfection 24 hours a day. A young woman with social phobia might overcome the belief that others are continually watching and harshly judging her.

This kind of therapy can help you overcome your tendency to put the worst possible interpretation on events or symptoms. Teens often imagine that the worst possible outcome is the thing that will happen. After evaluating the evidence for this belief and considering other possible outcomes, they might decide that the thing that is most likely to happen is quite different from what they thought had to happen. Then, they can develop new, alternative beliefs about their ability to handle a situation.

In CBT, a major part of eliminating damaging automatic thoughts is to evaluate the basis for a belief by asking if the objective evidence justifies it. Often life experiences don't support your automatic thought, and then you can find a more realistic belief to replace it. This is a challenging task, because changing the way you think can mean undoing years of negative automatic thought patterns.

So how do you figure out what your automatic thoughts are? Ask yourself: "What's the first thing that went through my mind when the scary situation occurred?" If you scream and run when you see a spider, your automatic thought might be "It's going to bite me and I'll die" or "It might be poisonous." The therapist will help you see that with this automatic thought, you're really making a generalization that all spiders are poisonous or all spiders will bite you. The first thought you have is that this is dangerous, and you don't have the resources to deal with it. Your automatic thought is saying, "I'm in this spider's space, it's going to bite me, poison me, and there's not a thing in the world I can do to prevent it from happening."

Your therapist will help you evaluate the truth of this statement. What do you know about spiders? Is it true that all spiders are poisonous and bite people? Of course not. In fact, in the United States, there are only two species that can be said to be poisonous, and it's not likely that either will kill you. And is it true that when anything gets near a spider it automatically springs and launches a deadly poison?

Again, no. The therapist will lead you in this logical vein. Well, if not all spiders are poisonous, and they don't bite everything in their path, the assumption you're making is not true.

You can then ask yourself:

> ▶ "What's the worst thing that could happen? *The spider would bite me and I'd die.*"
> ▶ "What would be the best that could happen? *The spider would run away and leave me alone.*"
> ▶ "What's the most likely thing? *The spider freezes or runs and hides.*"

The point of evaluating automatic thoughts is to figure out a more fact-based approach rather than rely on emotional thinking. Base your thinking on facts as much as possible. Once you do that, you can come up with a more accurate automatic thought: *"There's a spider. I don't like them very much. I won't disturb it, but it probably won't disturb me either."* If you take into consideration all the evidence, you'll see that most likely the spider won't bother you. By changing your thinking and reinforcing that new thought or belief, you'll be much less likely to feel anxious.

Behavior. The "behavioral" part of CBT focuses on changing your reactions to anxiety-provoking situations and handling the stress that comes with them. A key element of the behavioral part of treatment for many types of anxiety disorders is a method called *exposure.* Using exposure, your therapist will help you confront the very thing you fear.

Here's how it works: Let's say you have obsessive-compulsive disorder and you constantly wash your hands because you think they are contaminated. Using exposure, your therapist might encourage you to get your hands dirty and then wait for a certain amount of time without washing. Your therapist then would help you cope with the resulting anxiety you'd feel, sitting there with dirt on your hands. Eventually, after you've repeated this exercise many times, your anxiety will begin to diminish.

In another type of exposure exercise, people with social phobia might be encouraged to initiate conversations with people, express themselves openly in class, or offer to give a speech or spend time at a school dance, for example, without giving in to the temptation to flee. In some cases the individual might be asked to deliberately make slight social blunders and watch other's reactions; if they aren't as bad as the person expects, the social anxiety may begin to fade.

In a treatment session for panic disorder, the therapist may use a technique called *panic induction* in which panic symptoms are intentionally induced in the person with the disorder to prove to her that she won't die, pass out, or have a heart attack as a result.

During treatment, your therapist will probably assign "homework"—specific problems that you'll need to work on between sessions. Exposure will be carried out only when you're ready and will be done gradually and only with your permission. You'll work with the therapist to determine how much you can handle and at what pace you can proceed.

BEHAVIORAL THERAPY

Behavioral therapy alone, without a strong cognitive component, has been a popular method to treat specific phobias for many years. This method also involves exposure, so that the person is gradually exposed to the object or situation that is feared. At first, the exposure may be only through pictures or audiotapes or through the patient's ability to imagine the situation. Later, if possible, the person actually confronts the feared object or situation. Often the therapist goes along with the patient to provide support and guidance.

STRESS MANAGEMENT TECHNIQUES

Stress management techniques and meditation may help you keep calm and enhance the effects of therapy, although there isn't any scientific evidence yet to support the value of these approaches by themselves in helping people recover from anxiety disorders. Most mental health experts include some type of relaxation or breathing techniques as part of their CBT or behavioral methods, because learning to control breathing and relax muscles can help you control or prevent anxiety.

Relaxation training is a crucial part of stress management, because when you can relax your body you'll automatically reduce the harmful effects of stress. You'd be surprised how many kids think they know exactly how to relax, but when we say "relax," we don't mean lying on your bed with your iPod headphones clamped in your ears.

When we say "relax," we're referring to muscle relaxation and focusing your thoughts on something besides stressful thoughts for a time. As you do relaxation exercises, breathing slows, blood pressure drops, muscles relax, headaches fade away, and your anxiety lessens. You can see that the effects of relaxation are the exact opposite of the physical symptoms of anxiety. Since the definition of anxiety involves rapid breathing and pounding heartbeats, if you can control these physical symptoms you automatically control your anxiety.

BREATHING

Everybody breathes, right? Even babies can do it all on their own. But what you may not realize is that your breathing changes when you get anxious. At these times, you start to take shallow breaths, using your chest muscles to breathe in. This means that only the top part of your lungs will fill with air. When you're experiencing anxiety, here's what's probably happening: You start taking quick, shallow breaths. Alarm bells go off in your brain as your oxygen level falls. Stress chemicals pour into your bloodstream. The more stress chemicals, the more anxious you feel. As your anxiety grows, you breathe even more quickly and more shallowly, which lowers your oxygen level further. Do you see the vicious circle starting up here? When you're tense, have you ever felt lightheaded or anxious? That's the warning that you're breathing shallowly.

Here's another interesting fact—it is a physical impossibility to feel anxious and calm at the same time. So if you can control your breathing so that you are taking in air and letting it out calmly, it will be much harder to feel anxious. In fact, of anything you can do to ease anxiety, breathing in healthy, calm ways will probably produce the most dramatic results. That may be hard to believe—it seems so simple. It doesn't cost anything, and you can do it on your own, anywhere at any time.

Still not convinced? Try this simple exercise to see what happens when you are breathing incorrectly (breathing shallowly). You're going to have to lie down for this test.

1. Contract your stomach muscles as hard as you can. Really suck it in.
2. Inhale. Notice what your chest is doing—it's the only part of your body that is rising.
3. Notice that air only fills the upper portion of your lungs.
4. Now, relax your stomach muscles and breathe into your abdomen. In other words, puff up your stomach as far as it will go with air as you breathe in. See how the lower portion of your lungs fill up?

What you need to do is to learn how to breathe from your diaphragm, the dome-shaped muscle at the bottom of your lungs that helps breathing by moving up and down. You can feel your diaphragm by placing your hand over the area right below your lungs and above your belly button.

Here's how to start relaxation breathing:

1. Get into a comfortable position (either sitting or lying down).
2. Close your eyes.
3. Place your hands on your lap, and relax your arms.
4. Begin taking slow, deep breaths.
5. Breathe rhythmically from your diaphragm, not your chest.

DEEP BREATHING EXERCISE

To get even more bang for your buck, try taking your breathing to the next level by practicing deep breathing. But beware—it's hard for most people to do this all the time. You won't be expected to walk around in deep breathing mode on a regular basis. However, this technique does come in handy if you're just a bit anxious or tense. As a matter of fact, some people try this deep breathing exercise as a way of preventing anxiety, as they face a situation they know has caused them problems in the past. For example, if you have a lot of trouble giving a speech, practicing deep breathing before getting up in front of the auditorium may help control the butterflies. But deep breathing is also effective in controlling phobias and some of the most severe stress situations you'll encounter.

Find Your Diaphragm

To tell the difference between breathing from your chest and your diaphragm:

1. Lie down. Put your hand on your abdomen.

2. As you breathe in deeply and slowly, push your stomach out as you breathe (it's okay to look fat). Let your stomach rise about an inch as you breathe in.

3. Breathe out, and contract your abdomen. It should fall about an inch. Your chest will rise slightly at the same time.

4. Become aware of your stomach pushing out as you inhale and back in as you exhale.

5. Relax your stomach muscles. It's impossible to let your diaphragm move down if your stomach muscles are tight.

A word of reassurance: Deep breathing isn't magic or hypnosis, and it won't make you unconscious or out of control. You won't be transported into some alternative state of consciousness. You'll just be very relaxed, and you'll be breathing correctly. It can distract you or lessen anxiety.

Here's how to do it:

1. Sit in a chair with your back straight and your feet flat on the floor. Put your hands in your lap.
2. Breathe in through your nose without forcing. Let your stomach expand as air fills your abdomen.
3. In one big long breath, imagine that air is filling your chest and lungs with air. Allow your chest to fully expand, as your shoulders rise a bit. (Keep your shoulders relaxed, though.)
4. Imagine air is expanding your abdomen and chest in all directions.
5. Breathe out slowly through your nose. Breathing out should take longer than breathing in. Keep the breath slow and even (don't puff).
6. Breathe this way for at least one minute. Don't strain. Focus on keeping your breath even and slow and your body fully relaxed.

You can practice deep breathing any time. If you like to play sports, you can practice this a few minutes before taking a jump shot, or before serving in tennis. You can practice while you're sitting in the school bus or before a big exam.

BREATHING STRESS-BUSTERS

There are lots of variations on the breathing techniques. Try this countdown breathing exercise:

1. Inhale slowly, counting slowly from one to four: 1, 2, 3, 4.
2. As you breathe out, count more slowly back down: 4, 3, 2, 1.
3. Do this for several breaths or for as long as you want to.

For slightly more tense situations, enlarge on the countdown breathing exercise:

1. Inhale slowly, and think "10."
2. Breathe out.

3. Inhale and think "nine."
4. Exhale.
5. Keep counting down with each breath in. (If you start to feel dizzy, slow down.)
6. When you get to "zero," you should be feeling much calmer. If you aren't, start over at 10 and work your way down.

QUICK FIX BREATHING

If you're struggling with anxiety, you may need help from quick fix breathing. In the middle of an anxiety attack, focus on your breathing. Here's what to do:

1. Stop. Take several slow, deep breaths.
2. Return to normal breathing.
3. Take several more slow, deep breaths.

INVIGORATING YOURSELF

Some kids are not quite in touch with their internal bodies, and they may not even realize that they're feeling anxious. If you're one of these silent anxiety types, you may feel only tired or dragging in an anxiety-ridden situation. Working on certain breathing exercises can pull more oxygen into your body and invigorate you. The following breathing technique will provide you with the oxygen in the shortest time. Long-distance runners like this technique because it's good for all the breathing muscles (so if you're on the track team, you'll get a double benefit).

1. Breathe in slowly, using your diaphragm. Push your stomach out.
2. Breathe in again (without breathing out in between) while counting to four. Really push out that rib cage and your upper lungs.
3. Breathe out through your mouth for one count, pulling in your rib cage area.
4. Breathe out again to a count of four, really tucking in your ribs and contracting your abdominal muscles.
5. Squeeze out the carbon dioxide from the lower portion of your lungs.

Here's another good invigoration exercise. Don't try this if you have very high or very low blood pressure, an ear infection, or an eye infection. Do this one in sets of four to six breaths at a time.

1. Lie on your back with the soles of your feet close to your rump.
2. Close your eyes and focus on your stomach area.
3. Breathe in through your nose—short and explosive.
4. Breathe out through your nose—short and explosive—while strongly contracting your abdominal muscles.
5. Pump your lungs like a bellows. Both in and out breaths should be short and equal in length.

LEARN TO RELAX

Learning how to relax is equally important if you're going to conquer most kinds of anxiety. Your therapist will work with you to help you decide when to do relaxation exercises and will probably teach you some specific ways to relax. Here are some basic tips on relaxing that can help you no matter what type of anxiety disorder you have.

1. Find a position that feels comfortable and close your eyes.
2. Begin taking slow, deep breaths.
3. As you silently say the word relax, focus on the top of your head and consciously relax that part of your body. When you feel the top of your head relax, move down to the eye area, relaxing those muscles. Move on to the sinus area of your face.
4. Repeat the word relax as you consciously relax each muscle group. Don't move on until you can feel that area relax.
5. Move on to your ears and the back of your neck. This is the area that holds a lot of tension, so spend some time here. Don't move on until you can feel those muscles relax.
6. Move slowly down your body, all the way to your toes, relaxing muscles as you go.

PROGRESSIVE MUSCLE RELAXATION

Some kids have trouble mentally willing a muscle to relax. If you're having a problem with this, try progressive muscle relaxation:

1. Sit or lie down and close your eyes.
2. Begin taking slow, deep breaths.
3. Start with the muscles behind your neck. Firmly tense just those muscles, but keep the rest of your body relaxed.
4. Hold for five seconds and then relax those muscles. Visualize the muscle relaxing.

5. Now move on to the muscles of your shoulders. Tense those muscles, keeping the rest of your muscles in the body relaxed. Tighten the muscles as much as possible, hold for five seconds, and then relax.
6. If you have trouble tightening and relaxing muscles, practice first with your fist. Clench it tightly and then relax. That's what you should be doing with each of the muscle groups in your body.
7. If you have an injury or a weak muscle group, be careful when tensing that area. You might want to skip it altogether.

RELAXATION QUICKIE

It's great if you've got 20 minutes or so to relax. But sometimes you'll need to be able to relax more quickly than that. If you're sitting on stage ready to get up and give a presentation to the entire high school student body, you won't have time to think about relaxing. If you're phobic about dogs and you see one in the distance, you'll want some relaxation tips right away. As you feel the anxiety build, try these brief tips:

▶ This may sound corny, but think "love." Fill yourself with love—think about someone you love and allow yourself to experience fully how much you care about that person. This may take some practice, or you may find it easy to become a "love bubble." But remember, you can't experience two opposing strong feelings at the same time. Fear and love can't coexist.

▶ If thinking about love doesn't work, try something simpler: Think "happy." Force yourself to smile and think about a big cheery grin plastered all over your face. Say to yourself, "I'm so happy! I'm just fine." When you think "happy" and make your facial muscles smile, you may be surprised to find the anxiety lessening.

VISUALIZATION

Now that you've learned how to breathe and relax, the next step in dealing with anxiety is to practice visualization. Some kids are very good at this and find it fun; others have trouble "seeing with the mind's eye." It can be a very effective tool in relaxation and anxiety management, so at least give it a try.

Meditation is a fairly passive exercise—you're relaxed, you may concentrate on just one word or sound. You open your mind and let thoughts roll in or out. Visualization, however, is a much more active form of meditation. If you're the busy sort, and your mind is always jumping from one thought to the next, this may be easier for you to do since it requires your mind to be occupied with something.

You probably already know that some places are automatically stressful and others are automatically peaceful. If you imagine Grand Central Terminal at rush hour, with the clang of the trains and the roar of the crowds—that's pretty stressful. Compare that to a warm spring day in the mountains by a small, gentle waterfall. Maybe there are birds chirping or a gentle wind blowing. See the difference?

When you visualize, you're exploiting the fact that some places are just very relaxing. When you visualize, you're basically first relaxing yourself and then mentally imagining a calming scene. Some therapists call this your "happy place." It should be any place that's calming, that makes you feel good about being there, one you've visited or one that you imagined. It might be the ocean, a deserted island, a temple high in the Andes with the wind blowing, or a forest clearing. The better you are at imagining this scene, the stronger the experience will be. Try to imagine sounds, smells, and sensations. Try to feel the breeze on your skin, the sand under your feet, the sound of the water.

In *active visualization,* you can give yourself a positive suggestion (called an *affirmation*) when you're in your happy place. Here's how to visualize:

1. First, choose one of the relaxation techniques above and get totally relaxed. You can do this sitting down or lying down.
2. When you are fully relaxed, keep your eyes closed and imagine a calm, beautiful scene in full detail. You can choose a place you've been to or make one up in your mind.
3. Really experience the scene with as many senses as possible.
4. As you relax in your happy place, give yourself an affirmation. Remember to keep it positive: "I feel peaceful" or "I feel completely relaxed." You can be more specific if you like: "I feel completely relaxed in every social situation."
5. Remember to keep this positive. Don't say, "I want to stop being scared of dogs." Say, "I will feel pleasantly relaxed and calm whenever I see a dog."
6. When you're finished with your happy place, tell yourself, "When I open my eyes, I will feel calm, peaceful, and fully refreshed." Then slowly open your eyes.

You can use visualizations and affirmations to deal with anxiety, or you can prepare for a potentially anxious situation the same way. If you're preparing for something, you might want to move from your happy place to a scene of the upcoming anxious or stressful situation. Watch yourself confidently and calmly handling the situation. In essence, you're mentally practicing how to deal with this anxiety. The more chances you give yourself to preview such a situation, the more likely you'll be able to handle it more calmly.

Does this seem strange or weird? It's hard for some kids to understand how a simple picture in your mind could possibly affect the anxiety you feel. Visualization works because your brain can't tell the difference between something you've actually experienced and something you've intensely imagined. Professional or Olympic athletes use these methods every day to achieve peak performances in their sports. If it works for them, you can bet it will also work for you!

STRETCH YOUR ANXIETY AWAY

Sometimes you may be in an anxiety-provoking situation and you don't feel comfortable taking 10 minutes to close your eyes and practice your relaxation and visualization or breathing methods. You've got another alternative: stretching away the anxiety.

When you feel anxious or scared, you've probably learned by now how to identify changes throughout your body. One of those body-wide changes involves your muscles (especially in the abdominal area). Emotions such as fear, anxiety, resentment, and anger all can cause muscles to contract, knot up, and tighten. Stretching forces these muscles to relax, which can help make you feel relaxed all over. Not every teenager reacts to anxiety in the same physical way. Terry gets a stiff neck. Kate experiences back spasms. Tasha says her stomach knots up. But in all these cases, the body expresses the emotions these teens feel. If you're standing up at the podium with a death grip on the corners of the stand, with your jaw clenched, your head pounding, and your stomach turning over, odds are you're not feeling relaxed and happy.

The good news is that you can get rid of a lot of this anxiety expressed as physical tension by stretching the tense area. If you combine the stretching with some of the deep breathing techniques you learned earlier, you'll be surprised how much less anxious you'll feel. The best thing about stretching is that the techniques work when you're already anxious, but they also work to prevent you from getting anxious and keyed up.

In a perfect world, you'd stop and stretch about every half hour, but who has time for that during a busy school day? Alternatively, you can time your stretch breaks for the beginning of the school day (during homeroom or morning meeting), at mid-morning break if you have one, during lunch, mid-afternoon break, and during study time at night.

STRETCHING AT THE COMPUTER OR YOUR DESK

Periodic stretching while you're hunched over your computer for hours on end is so important that some programs will periodically chime, flash an icon on your computer, and display stretching exercises on your screen to remind you! Alternatively, you can just take some time out every so often for the following.

Neck rolls. The back of the neck is a favorite place for tension to build up. Follow this technique to stretch this vulnerable area:

1. Pull your shoulders up to your ears.
2. Rotate your head and neck in large circles, three times going counterclockwise, three times clockwise. Go slowly.
3. If you find that rotating your head this way hurts, try drawing an imaginary circle in front of your face with your nose. (It may sound weird, but this allows you to rotate your neck without the head tilt that some people find painful.)

Chest expander. This one helps with your breathing.

1. Lean forward from your hips and clasp your hands behind your back.
2. Continue to lean forward and inhale while lifting your arms up behind you. This will lift and open your chest.
3. Hold for a count of three.
4. Lower your arms and take a complete breath.
5. Repeat two times.

Shoulder scrunches. If you experience tension in your back muscles, here's a good technique to relax this area:

1. With your right hand, grab your left arm just below the elbow.
2. Pull your elbow toward your right shoulder.
3. Hold for three breaths.
4. Repeat on the other side.

Here's an alternative one:

1. Rotate your shoulder in a large circle.
2. Bring your shoulder blades together and lift your shoulders toward your ears as high as possible.
3. Curl your shoulders forward.
4. Pull your shoulders down toward the floor.
5. Rotate your shoulders slowly, three times in each direction.

Stretch your spine. As anxiety builds, you may feel stiff and tense throughout your back area. Try these stretches to ease the anxiety buildup:

1. Sit down and place your feet flat on the floor.
2. Lean forward, relaxing your neck, shoulders, and back.
3. Rest your chest on your thigh and let your hands drop down to the carpet.
4. Hold for a count of three.
5. Curl your spine as you sit back up.

Here's another antianxiety spine stretch aimed at loosening the muscles in the lower back:

1. Sit up straight so that your back doesn't touch the chair.
2. Cross your legs at the thigh.
3. Put your hand on the outside of the opposite thigh and the other hand on the back of your chair.
4. Look over your shoulder.
5. Sit straight and tall, lifting your chest and pulling down your shoulders.
6. Take three deep breaths.
7. Turn forward and repeat on the other side.

OTHER SELF-HELP WAYS TO EASE ANXIETY

While you're working with your therapist, maybe taking medication, and learning how to do your relaxation exercises and breathe, there are still other things you can do on your own to ease some of the anxiety in your life. Many of these may sound pretty simple, but you'll be surprised at how well they work.

Listen to music. This one probably isn't hard for most teens to do—you probably already carry music everywhere you go. But did you know that scientists have discovered that listening to music can slow your heart rate and reduce stress and anxiety? Of course, the type of music has an influence on how calming your body finds it. Even if you really like loud music or rap, in order to get a relaxation response, you need to choose quiet, soothing tones. Slow music is more soothing than fast, strings and woodwinds are more calming than discordant electronic sounds, and instrumentals are better than songs with words (too distracting).

Steam away anxiety. If you're feeling very nervous or anxious, try taking a hot, steamy shower, a bath, or a dip in a hot tub. Some scientists believe that the hot water prompts the release of chemicals in the brain that help you feel relaxed; the hot water will also help your muscles relax.

Pets to the rescue. As long as your anxiety or phobia is not pet-related, you should experience significant relaxation when petting a dog or cat or watching tropical fish. The simple act of stroking an animal reduces blood pressure in both humans and the pet—so you're doing both of you a favor!

Watch comedy. Did you know that laughing provides the same benefits as aerobic exercise—it lowers your blood pressure. It also can distract you from situations or thoughts you may find stressful. If you're feeling anxious and keyed up, try relaxing with an old *Friends* or *Seinfeld* DVD or video, go to a comedy club, or read something humorous.

WHAT TO AVOID DURING TREATMENT

Caffeine, illicit drugs, and even some over-the-counter cold medications can worsen your anxiety symptoms. The caffeine in several cans of cola or a couple of cups of coffee can make you feel jittery or keyed up. Some over-the-counter medications can do the same thing. Check with your physician or pharmacist before taking any additional medicines, and ask if they can make anxiety worse.

Sweet, fat-rich candy can do the same thing. You might think you're eating to relax, but the fat in many types of chocolate will slow down the benefits of the sugar. That means it may take up to an hour for that high-fat candy to help you relax.

If you smoke (and for your health, we hope you don't), you may think it helps you relax. In the very short term, nicotine *can* have that effect. But it doesn't take a long time before the poisons in the smoke boost your heart rate and start to stress your entire body. Don't believe it? Take this test:

1. Before you get out of bed, take your pulse.
2. Smoke your morning cigarette.
3. Take your pulse again.

Voila! That's your heart on nicotine, and it isn't pretty. Every time you light up, every time you breathe in that smoke, your heart is speeding up. For anyone prone to anxiety or fear, that's an added stress you could do without.

NATURAL DIET-RELATED RELAXERS

Anything you can do to keep anxiety at bay in your everyday life will help you manage anxiety disorders. Eating a healthy, well-balanced diet can help ease anxiety. In addition, however, science has discovered that both sugar and starch (when not accompanied by fat) can help you relax by helping the chemical tryptophan enter the brain, where it's converted to the calming chemical serotonin. Sugar can help you relax within about five minutes; starches take about 30 minutes.

MEDICATIONS

Medication is just one of many treatment options to manage symptoms of anxiety disorders. It can give you a short-term boost to help while you heal yourself. Medications don't cure the problem itself any more than a Band-Aid heals a cut; your body can heal itself, given

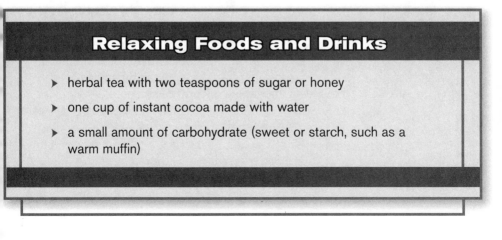

Relaxing Foods and Drinks

➤ herbal tea with two teaspoons of sugar or honey

➤ one cup of instant cocoa made with water

➤ a small amount of carbohydrate (sweet or starch, such as a warm muffin)

the right support. Medications can keep your symptoms under control and help you lead a normal, fulfilling life as you work on your problems with your therapist.

Some teenagers (or their parents) believe that taking medications means you're weak, and they don't want to be dependent on a pill. As a result, sometimes these people don't take their medications; or they take too little of the drug, mistakenly believing that less is better; or they take it in fits and starts as they think of it. Some kids stop taking an effective medication too quickly, assuming that they are cured.

When psychiatrists or other physicians prescribe medications for anxiety disorders, they often work closely with psychologists, social workers, or counselors who provide psychotherapy to determine the precise nature of your treatment. (In New Mexico and Louisiana, specially trained medical psychologists can now legally prescribe medication.) It's important to remember that there is one specific dose that is best for you, and your physician will help identify what that amount may be. You can cause more (or different) symptoms if you take your medication irregularly or abruptly stop it altogether without the advice of your doctor. The medication needs a chance to work. Far too many teens give up on their medication after a couple of days. Taking a pill for an anxiety disorder is not like taking an aspirin for a headache. It won't work right away. It may take up to a month before you see your symptoms improve.

Work with your doctor in the beginning of your treatment as he or she adjusts the dose gradually. Most physicians will begin a drug at a

If Your Doctor Recommends Medication

► Tell your doctor about all alternative therapies, herbs, and over-the-counter medications you use.

► Ask about the effects and side effects of the drug.

► Ask what happens if the drug is stopped. (Some drugs can't safely be stopped abruptly; they must be tapered slowly under your doctor's supervision.)

low dose and then increase it slowly according to your response. You must take a drug for several weeks at full dose to figure out whether it works.

Once your symptoms are under control, your doctor will probably suggest that you taper your medication. This might take anywhere from a few weeks to 12 to 18 months, depending on your condition. As you gradually stop taking your medications, some of your symptoms may return. After about one month, your doctor will assess how well you're handling the stress and anxiety without medication. If it's not going well, you can always discuss taking the drug again or trying a different one. Sometimes a doctor may decide that long-term medication is the best treatment.

There are several classes of effective medications for anxiety disorders. The most common is a class of antidepressants called selective serotonin reuptake inhibitors (SSRIs). A number of medications that were originally approved for treatment of depression also are effective in treating anxiety disorders. Tricyclic antidepressants (such as imipramine) and benzodiazepines (such as lorazepam) are less commonly used in the treatment of childhood anxiety disorders. Other medications have been used to treat anxiety disorders in adults but require further study in children and adolescents.

Selective serotonin reuptake inhibitors (SSRIs). SSRIs are currently the medications of choice for the treatment of both childhood and adult anxiety disorders; experts believe that SSRIs work most of the time for most of the teens for whom they are prescribed. This group of medications includes fluoxetine (Prozac), sertraline (Zoloft), paroxetine (Paxil), fluvoxamine (Luvox), citalopram (Celexa), and escitalopram (Lexapro). The U.S. Food and Drug Administration (FDA) has specifically approved the use of certain SSRIs (Prozac, Zoloft, and Luvox) and the tricyclic antidepressant clomipramine (Anafranil) for the treatment of obsessive-compulsive disorder in kids. Doctors commonly use SSRIs to treat kids with other anxiety disorders as well, based on careful studies that have discovered improvement in symptoms and medication safety in children with anxiety disorders. Such controlled studies give the FDA the facts needed to determine whether medications should be approved, but unfortunately, studies into the use of these medications in children aren't done as often as for adults. Many medications not specifically approved by the FDA for treating a specific illness may still legally be prescribed by your doctor if he or she has reason to believe they may help your particular symptoms. (This is called off-label prescribing, and doctors do it all the time.)

Although the SSRIs are technically antidepressants and were originally approved for treating depression, it turns out that they are just as effective in treating anxiety disorders. If your doctor prescribes an antidepressant, you'll need to take it for several weeks before your symptoms start to improve. It's important not to get discouraged and stop taking these medications before they've had a chance to work. Typically, these medications are started at a low dose and gradually increased until they reach a therapeutic level.

SSRIs are commonly prescribed for OCD, PTSD, and social phobia. SSRIs also are often used to treat people who have panic disorder in combination with OCD, social phobia, or depression. Venlafaxine, a drug closely related to the SSRIs, is useful for treating generalized anxiety disorder. Lexapro and Paxil are also indicated for GAD. Other newer antidepressants are under study for anxiety disorders, although one (bupropion [Wellbutrin]) doesn't seem to be effective for these conditions.

The SSRIs boost levels of a brain chemical messenger called serotonin. SSRIs have fewer side effects than older antidepressants, and those symptoms usually disappear with time. An adjustment in dosage or a switch to another SSRI will usually correct problems that continue. It's important to discuss side effects with your doctor so you won't be upset if you experience an uncomfortable reaction. The most common side effects are headache, nausea, and sleep problems. Of course, each of these symptoms also could be related to anxiety (e.g., headache or stomachache) and may improve with treatment of the anxiety disorder. Your doctor should review the symptoms of possible side effects with you and your parents before starting an SSRI and at subsequent follow-up visits.

Also, try not to expect instant results. You may notice that some of your symptoms begin to improve after a week or so, although some people may take up to four to six weeks to experience a significant response. Most doctors would expect to continue treatment with an SSRI for anxiety for about a year. If your symptoms come back, your doctor may recommend further medication treatment. However, just because you may be asked to take an SSRI now doesn't mean you'll be on medication for the rest of your life. Many kids with anxiety disorders only need one course of medication.

Tricyclics. This older class of antidepressants has been more widely studied in the treatment of anxiety disorders than SSRIs. For anxiety disorders other than OCD, they are equally as effective as the SSRIs, but many physicians and patients prefer the newer drugs because the tricyclics sometimes cause dizziness, drowsiness, dry mouth, and weight gain. Tricyclics include

> ‣ amitriptyline (Elavil)
> ‣ clomipramine (Anafranil)
> ‣ desipramine (Norpramin, Pertofrane)
> ‣ doxepin (Sinequan or Adapin)
> ‣ imipramine (Tofranil)
> ‣ nortriptyline (Aventyl or Pamelor)
> ‣ trazodone (Desyrel)

Tricyclics are useful in treating teens with a combination of an anxiety disorder and depression. Those especially helpful in treating panic include imipramine, desipramine, nortriptyline, amitriptyline, doxepin, and clomipramine. Those helpful in generalized anxiety include imipramine. Those especially good for OCD include clomipramine. Social anxiety responds especially well to venlafaxine (an SNRI).

Monoamine oxidase inhibitors (MAOIs). These drugs are the oldest class of antidepressant medications. The most commonly prescribed MAOI is phenelzine (Nardil), which is helpful for people with panic disorder and social phobia. Tranylcypromine (Parnate) is also used to treat anxiety disorders.

Anyone taking MAOIs must follow a special restrictive diet to avoid interactions with some foods and beverages, including cheese and red wine, which contains a chemical called tyramine. However, the new transdermal MAOI Emsam poses less concern about dietary restrictions.

MAOIs also interact with some other medications, including SSRIs. Interactions between MAOIs and other substances can cause a dangerous spike in blood pressure, along with other potentially life-threatening reactions.

Antianxiety medications. High-potency benzodiazepines relieve symptoms quickly and have few side effects, although you may feel a bit sleepy. However, in children and adolescents, benzodiazepines often have the opposite effect. Because people can develop a tolerance to these drugs (which means you'd have to take higher and higher doses to get the same effect), benzodiazepines are generally only prescribed for short periods of time. However, antianxiety medications for panic disorder may be taken for six months to a year. If you've had problems with drug or alcohol abuse in the past, it's not likely that your doctor will prescribe these medications, because you may become dependent on them. Benzodiazepines include

- alprazolam (Xanax): panic, generalized anxiety, phobias, social phobias
- chlordiazepoxide (Librium): generalized anxiety, phobias
- clonazepam (Klonopin): panic, phobias, social phobia
- diazepam (Valium): generalized anxiety, panic, phobias
- lorazepam (Ativan): generalized anxiety, panic, phobias
- oxazepam (Serax): generalized anxiety, phobias

If you have panic, your doctor may prescribe Xanax, Klonopin, Valium, or Ativan. If you have phobias, you may receive Xanax, Klonopin, Ativan, Serax, or Librium. Social phobia responds best to Xanax or Klonopin. For generalized anxiety, you may receive Xanax, Valium, Ativan, Serax, or Librium.

Buspirone, a member of a class of drugs called azipirones, is an antianxiety medication that is used to treat GAD. Possible side effects include dizziness, headaches, and nausea. Unlike the benzodiazepines, buspirone must be taken consistently for at least two weeks to achieve an antianxiety effect.

You should not suddenly stop taking benzodiazepines without talking to your doctor, because you could experience withdrawal symptoms. Instead, reducing the dosage gradually can avoid those symptoms. In some cases, the symptoms of anxiety can return after these medications are stopped. Because of these potential problems with benzodiazepines, some physicians hesitate to use them or use them in inadequate doses, even when they are of potential benefit to the patient.

Beta blockers.   Propanolol (Inderal) or atenolol (Tenormin) represent a type of drug called beta blockers that are often used to treat heart conditions. However, they also can ease symptoms of certain anxiety disorders (particularly social phobia).

If you can predict an anxious situation ahead of time (such as flying in a plane or giving a speech), your doctor may prescribe a beta blocker, which can keep your heart from pounding, your hands from shaking, and other physical symptoms from developing. However, anyone with asthma shouldn't take beta blockers, because they can trigger an asthma attack.

Side effects.   It's possible to experience side effects from almost any medication. Usually these side effects are minor; they may be irritating, but they don't require medical attention. These side effects may also diminish or end in a few days or weeks as your body adjusts to the medication.

Before using one of these medications, ask your doctor what you can expect, what might get better as time passes, and which side effects you need to report immediately.

Some doctors are reluctant to discuss side effects, because it's hard to know which patients will experience them, and doctors worry that bringing up the subject may make you more inclined to experience side effects. On the other hand, if you don't know what to expect, any side effects can be scary. If you know what to expect, you can prepare yourself to deal with it.

For example, common side effects of many drugs (including tricyclic antidepressants) include dry mouth, blurred close vision, or constipation. Often these minor problems improve over a few weeks as your body adjusts or if the dosage is lowered. In the meantime, you can handle these effects by sucking on a hard candy for dry mouth, getting a new eyeglass prescription for blurred vision, and eating more bran and fruits and vegetables to combat constipation.

Suicide risk. You may have heard about recent concerns linking certain antidepressants with teenage suicide attempts. The FDA issued a warning in October 2004 that antidepressant medications (including SSRIs) may increase suicidal thoughts and suicide attempts in a small number of children and adolescents. This caution was based on review of 24 brief studies of nine antidepressants involving more than 4,400 children and adolescents with major depressive disorder, obsessive-compulsive disorder, and other psychiatric disorders. The studies showed that the average risk of suicidal thoughts and attempts occurred in 4 percent of patients treated with an antidepressant, compared with 2 percent of patients treated with a sugar pill. No actual suicides occurred in any of the studies.

There was some evidence that suicidal thoughts and behaviors occurred most often at the beginning of treatment or when the dosage was changed. However, this doesn't mean that a problem couldn't appear later in treatment.

The FDA warning does not forbid use of these medications; it's just an alert to the risk of suicidal thoughts and behavior as a side effect. However, the FDA also notes that this risk must be weighed against the need for the medication in the first place. When you start taking any new medication, you and your parents should be on the lookout for any changes in your thinking, emotions, or behaviors (especially suicidal thoughts).

Newer studies further refine this information. A 2006 study concludes that youths who use certain antidepressants—but not most SSRIs—are more likely to attempt suicide, according to the report in the August *Archives of General Psychiatry*. In that study, researchers found that those who had attempted suicide were 1.5 times more likely to have been taking an antidepressant, and they were 15 times more likely to die in the attempt than those not treated with an antidepressant. In particular, kids who used antidepressants seemed to be at higher risk for suicide in the period after being hospitalized, especially if they were just starting antidepressants. However, not all types of antidepressants carried the same risk.

Venlafaxine (Effexor)—a serotonin-norepinephrine reuptake inhibitor (SNRI)—was associated with 2.3 times the risk of suicide attempts compared with no drug treatment at all. Tricyclic antidepressants were also significantly linked with suicide attempts. But with the exception of Zoloft, SSRIs weren't linked to suicide attempts, the study found.

In any case, if you're taking any type of antidepressant and you begin having suicidal thoughts or suddenly feel agitated, restless, or irritable, you should tell your parents and contact your doctor immediately. The medication dose may need to be lowered or changed. You shouldn't stop taking your medication without a doctor's supervision since this may worsen symptoms.

SUPPORT GROUPS

In addition to therapy, many teenagers join a support group, where they can share their problems and successes with other kids having similar anxiety problems. If you've been feeling like the only kid on the planet with these symptoms or annoying problems, you'll be amazed to find out how many others are in the same situation. It can be very comforting to find out that other kids have experienced similar issues, and you'll probably be amazed to find so many kids who are going through exactly what you're dealing with. Many kids with anxiety disorders feel terribly alone; participating in a self-help group can help you see that you aren't the only one with these problems. An effective group can help members recover by offering mutual support, tips on coping, and the most current information about causes and treatment and by eliminating some of the myths about anxiety disorders.

Your mental health expert may be able to refer you to a good group. You also can find a state-by-state list of support groups by visiting the Web site of the Anxiety Disorders Association of America at http://www.adaa.org/GettingHelp/SupportGroups.asp.

OUTLOOK

All treatments for anxiety disorders—whether that's CBT, individual therapy, group therapy, medication, behavioral techniques, or relaxation exercises—work to support your understanding that you are the person who can control your body and your life. Treatments are highly effective and can greatly improve the quality of your life.

WHAT YOU NEED TO KNOW

- An anxiety disorder is a real emotional disturbance and not a moral failing, and it can be treated so that you can go on to have a healthy and full life.
- Before beginning treatment, your doctor will conduct a careful diagnostic evaluation to determine that your symptoms are due to an anxiety disorder, which anxiety disorders you may have, and what other conditions or issues you may have at the same time.
- If you've got one anxiety disorder, it's not unusual to have another type of anxiety disorder or a different mental health problem as well.
- If you've recovered from an anxiety disorder and it comes back after a time, recurrences can be treated just as effectively as the first episode.
- Psychotherapy for anxiety disorders involves either changing your behavior (behavioral therapy) or changing your thoughts and your behavior (cognitive-behavioral therapy, or CBT).
- The aim of both CBT and behavioral therapy is to ease your anxiety by eliminating your beliefs or behaviors that reinforce your anxiety disorder.
- In addition to therapy, you may be helped by a variety of relaxation techniques including meditation, muscle relaxation, breathing techniques, visualization, listening to music, watching a comedy, or taking a bath.
- You should avoid caffeine, illicit drugs, smoking, and even some over-the-counter cold medications that can worsen your anxiety symptoms.
- Eating a healthy, well-balanced diet can help ease anxiety.
- Medication can give you a short-term boost to help while you heal yourself.
- Medications used to treat anxiety include selective serotonin reuptake inhibitors (SSRIs), tricyclic antidepressants, and benzodiazepines.

➤ Because of a slight link between some antidepressants and suicide in teens, if you begin having suicidal thoughts or suddenly feel agitated, restless, or irritable, you should tell your parents and contact your doctor immediately.

➤ In addition to therapy, many teenagers join a support group, where they can share their problems and successes with other kids having similar anxiety problems.

"Am I Just Shy?":
Social Phobia

Sonja was a 17-year-old college student who developed such severe anxiety in social situations after her freshman year that she dreaded going back to school. In fact, her anxiety had reached the point that she thought seriously of quitting. Speaking up in class had become unbearable, and her very low self-esteem made her feel awkward and constantly worried about saying or doing the wrong thing and humiliating herself in front of others. Her fears were so pronounced that she'd never had a boyfriend, but her habit of dressing in bizarre ways probably didn't help her attract boys or make friends either.

With the help of a psychologist, Sonja worked on her self-esteem and discussed how to dress and how to handle herself in social situations. After discussions about negative self-talk and role playing, she eventually returned to college in the fall and continued to work on her issues on her own. Sonja has a type of social phobia known as general social phobia, or pathological shyness.

Ted, on the other hand, didn't have much of a problem in social situations. He enjoyed going to parties and meeting new people. But when he had to stand up at school and address the entire student body—more than 2,000 kids—he thought his heart was going to explode. As he stood in front of the podium, his hands were shaking, his heart was pounding, and perspiration poured down his back. His stomach was in knots, and he knew that when he opened his mouth, everyone would know how terrified he was by the shakiness of his voice. In fact, he wasn't entirely sure he would be able to speak at all.

Ted has a type of social phobia known as performance anxiety (also called stage fright) that directly affects his life. He refused to run for class president because he knew it would mean he'd have to give speeches and get up in front of the school.

If you have problems like Sonja or Ted, you may not be surprised to hear how many teenagers are so consumed with self-doubt and anxieties that they have trouble performing in front of others or making friends, let alone going out on a date. For these teens, just getting through the day can be tough, and eventually some become so crippled with anxieties that they are unable to leave the house.

Social anxiety is the third most common psychological problem in the United States today, affecting 15 million Americans a year. Unlike some other psychological problems, social anxiety is not well understood, even by doctors, who may often misdiagnose the condition. Most typically, social phobia develops in childhood or the mid- to late teen years, and affects guys and girls equally. Many kids with social phobia don't talk about it, because they figure as uncomfortable as they are in social situations, it would be even worse if others knew how they felt.

Social anxiety affects people like 15-year-old Janine, who loves clothes but hates to go shopping because she's convinced everyone is watching her. She knows it's not really true, but she can't get rid of the feeling that others might be looking at her as she stands in front of the three-way mirror trying on clothes. She worries that they're thinking she's too fat for that dress or that the color is wrong for her. She dreads having to talk to a sales clerk and prefers shopping in stores where there aren't many employees to ask her if she needs help. She's sure she's making a fool of herself when she goes shopping, her hands start to sweat, and she feels like bolting from the store.

Most adolescents feel socially awkward at times, but some teens are so anxious about being judged by others or behaving in a way that might cause embarrassment or ridicule that they learn to avoid social situations. Their fears are so pronounced that they are diagnosed with what is called a social phobia (also called social anxiety disorder).

For some kids, having a social phobia means they can't eat in public or write their name if someone is watching. A teenager with a social phobia might feel scared of talking to a teacher or might be afraid of getting up in front of the class and leaving the room when he or she needs to go to the bathroom. If you have a social phobia, you might find it almost impossible to get up in speech class and give a presentation. It might even be tough for you to enjoy a birthday party or sleeping over at a friend's house. Hosting your own parties can be almost impossible for teens with a social phobia.

SHYNESS V. SOCIAL PHOBIA

A true social phobia is much more than just normal shyness, simple "butterflies" before a presentation, or the awkward feelings most teens have from time to time. It's extreme shyness accompanied by anxiety that interferes with your life and makes you avoid doing things you might otherwise like to do. Although most kids are probably a little nervous about giving a speech in class or talking to a teacher, a teenager with a social phobia gets so terrified even thinking about doing these things that he can't function.

"I'd get terrified before any social situation," says Paul, a 15-year-old high school sophomore. "The closer I'd get to a party, the sicker inside I'd feel. By the time I got to the door, my heart was pounding and my palms were sweaty. I'd feel like I was standing apart from everyone else, and that they were all looking at me and thinking I was weird."

Things only went from bad to worse for Paul as he continued to try, on his own, to get over his phobia. "I remember I went to a party with a friend of mine, and it got so bad I couldn't stand it. My friend was sitting around laughing and joking with everyone. I felt totally out of place. I left the room and ended up hiding in the front hall closet. It was the only place I could breathe.

"When I came out of the closet, I still couldn't think of anything to say to anybody, so I went outside and sat down in a lawn chair. The host's brother, who had schizophrenia and didn't speak, came over and sat down next to me. We both sat there in the dark, in silence. But I felt totally relaxed with this guy because I knew he was more messed up than I was, and he didn't expect me to chat."

HOW YOU KNOW IF YOU HAVE IT

If you feel overwhelming anxiety and excessive self-consciousness during everyday social situations, you may have social phobia. Teens with social phobia have a persistent, intense, and chronic fear of being watched and judged by others and being embarrassed or humiliated by their own actions. Their fear may be so severe that it interferes with class or after-school activities. They may realize that their fear of being around other people is unreasonable, but they still can't stop feeling that way. They may worry for days or weeks before a dreaded situation is slated to occur.

Social phobia may be limited to only one type of situation, such as a fear of eating, drinking, or writing in front of others, or it may take the form of performance anxiety, centered around speaking or performing in public. In its most severe form, the social anxiety may be so generalized that you experience symptoms almost any time you're around other people. Some people, for example, can't write in public because they fear people are watching. Others have a horror of speaking up in class or talking to a teacher about a problem. Some people with social anxiety feel that a certain part of their body (such as their nose) is particularly odd looking and that everyone is staring at it.

The one symptom that everyone with social phobia has in common is that they know their fear is irrational. They recognize that others aren't really staring at them all the time, just waiting for them to make a mistake, and that people aren't intentionally trying to embarrass them. Yet no matter how clearly they understand this, they still have the same anxious symptoms.

Often this turns into a vicious circle. The more that teenagers with social phobia worry about experiencing the symptoms, the greater the likelihood of developing symptoms. They worry that they'll say something wrong, and they get so nervous and uptight that they do end up blurting out something that sounds a bit odd. People may react to their discomfort, and then they feel even worse.

Social phobia can interfere with your life. To avoid scary, panicky reactions, kids often rearrange their lives to dodge whatever situations set off their symptoms. At its worst, it can keep them from going to school or even leaving the house. Many teens with this problem have a hard time making and keeping friends, and dating may be out of the question.

Physical symptoms. Physical symptoms that often accompany the intense anxiety include blushing, sweating, trembling, racing

Selective Mutism

A few teens are so terribly shy or fearful about talking to others that they refuse to speak at all in class, to certain people, or in certain social situations. This is a type of social phobia called *selective mutism.* Kids who feel too anxious to talk because of social phobia can have completely normal conversations with people they feel comfortable with, such as their parents or their best friend—but other situations make them feel so uncomfortable they can't speak at all.

heartbeat, stomach discomfort, dizziness, nausea, the urge to cry, and difficulty speaking. You may be painfully embarrassed by these physical symptoms and worried that everybody's eyes are focused on you.

Psychological symptoms. Teens with social phobia may feel extreme discomfort, passivity, or hesitation when they are the center of attention. They may avoid starting conversations, performing, calling classmates on the phone for needed information, or ordering food in restaurants. They may not interact much with their classmates; typically, they're the kids on the outskirts of the group or standing alone at lunch or in the library. These teens typically avoid eye contact or mumble when speaking to others, and worry all the time about being evaluated, embarrassed, or humiliated. Speaking in public, reading aloud, or being called on in class is agonizing for them.

If this sounds like you, you may know that your feelings are irrational, but even if you manage to confront what you fear, you probably feel very anxious beforehand and intensely uncomfortable throughout. Afterward, the unpleasant feelings may linger, as you worry about how you may have been judged or what others may have thought about you.

Tom would love to have lots of friends, but he resists ever going to social events even though he's desperately lonely. Instead, he never goes anywhere because he's scared to meet new people. He worries, Will they like him? Will he think of anything to say? Maybe they'll just walk away or think he's stupid. Crowds of strangers are torture for him. "I'm never going to have friends," he thinks to himself. "I'll always be an outcast." As a result, he spends most weekends alone at home, watching TV with his parents and feeling miserable.

If you have social phobia, you probably feel uncomfortable even when you're around people you know, because you're always worrying that other kids are noticing everything you do and say, and making silent negative judgments about you.

CAUSE

Some teens are more likely to have problems with social anxiety than others, which is probably related to some combination of brain function, heredity, learned behaviors, and personality.

Brain function. Some scientists suspect that a brain problem involving the amygdala, an area of the brain involved in fear, may be somehow linked to social phobia.

Could This Be You?

Do you . . .

- have an intense, persistent fear that people are judging you?
- worry that you'll be humiliated by something you do?
- fear that people will notice you blushing, sweating, trembling, or being scared?
- know that your anxiety is excessive or unreasonable?

Does the feared social situation make you . . .

- always feel anxious?
- do anything to avoid participating in the feared situation?
- feel suddenly overcome by intense fear or discomfort?

During a feared social situation, do you have any of these symptoms?

- pounding heart
- sweating
- trembling or shaking
- shortness of breath
- choking
- chest pain
- nausea or stomach pains
- weak knees
- dizziness
- feelings of unreality or being detached from yourself
- fear of losing control or going crazy
- fear of dying
- numbness or tingling sensations
- chills or hot flushes

Genetics. If your parents or close relatives have anxiety problems, you'll be more likely to develop a problem with anxiety too. Many teens with social phobia have at least one parent who has similar problems. This could be because you've inherited certain biological traits from your parents that may affect the function of brain chemicals (including serotonin) that regulate things like anxiety, shyness, nervousness, and stress reactions.

For example, let's say you have experienced an embarrassing event—maybe you got up to give a speech and forgot what you wanted to say and the class laughed at you. If you were born with a genetic pattern that predisposes you to social phobia, that experience could sear itself into your brain as a traumatic event. After that speech and the traumatic reaction, you could develop a social phobia about speaking again in public.

Personality. It's also possible to develop social phobia if you were born with a cautious personality style and a tendency to be shy in new situations, or if you learned a cautious style because of past experiences, the way others reacted to you, or behaviors you learned from your family. Low self-confidence and a lack of ability to handle normal stress can also play a role in social phobia. If you tend to be a worrier or a perfectionist, you may also be more likely to develop social phobia.

Fight-or-flight. If you have social phobia, when you find yourself in certain social situations where you're afraid others are going to judge you, your body undergoes a series of physical changes that typically include sweating, rapid heartbeat, shortness of breath, faintness, and blushing. In more severe cases, you can have a panic reaction and become so overwhelmed with anxiety that you feel completely disoriented.

These symptoms are triggered by your body's built-in fight-or-flight alarm system that goes off at the wrong time. Some kids feel as if they're losing control, that they're going to do something stupid to embarrass themselves. They can feel so scared or panicked that they think they're going to die.

COEXISTING CONDITIONS

If you have social phobia, it's quite possible that you also may have another anxiety disorder. Some teens with social phobia also have depression; some abuse drugs or alcohol in an attempt to make themselves feel better in social situations. It's not unusual to experiment with drugs and alcohol during adolescence, especially if you're already feeling anxious in social situations. Being intensely uncomfortable at a party, for example, some teenagers try to relax themselves by drinking or using drugs. Although this may seem to make you feel less anxious or more outgoing at the time, it isn't a good solution. Drugs and alcohol create a false sense of security and relaxation that can ultimately make it even harder to function. They're also illegal and can lead to other problems and endanger your health. Taking drugs or drinking won't help you learn how to handle social situations or cure the underlying anxiety problem, and eventually it will only make matters worse.

TREATMENT

Fortunately, social phobia almost always can be treated successfully with carefully targeted cognitive-behavioral therapy, assertiveness training, and social skills training. In severe cases, medications may be required. The sad thing is that so many kids—and adults as well, for that matter—wait years before getting help. Many people don't realize they truly have a disorder, or they're too embarrassed to ask for help. Others don't realize that there's anything that can address the problem.

With the help of a trained cognitive-behavioral therapist, you can learn to manage your social phobia by developing coping skills to handle your anxiety. This involves understanding and adjusting thoughts and beliefs that help create the anxiety, practicing social skills to increase your confidence, and then gradually practicing these skills in real situations.

Cognitive behavioral therapy. Short-term cognitive-behavioral therapy is the only treatment that has been shown to work effectively and that can produce long-lasting, permanent relief from your anxieties. Fortunately, you won't need to spend years working with a therapist; positive, significant change can occur in as little as 12 sessions, although it's more likely to require between 16 and 24.

In the cognitive part of this therapy, your therapist will try to correct your catastrophic perceptions of what others think about you and help you understand what the actual consequences would be if you were less than perfect. This is called *cognitive restructuring.* You'll learn how to identify your misjudgments and develop more realistic expectations of the likelihood of danger in social situations. It's a gentle approach, in which you gradually face your worry thoughts step by step.

You might learn how to correct harmful "self-talk" that leads to anxiety by learning more positive self-talk that makes you feel more confident. Your therapist can focus on how you're thinking in certain situations and help you modify certain worry thoughts. To help you put things in perspective, a therapist may ask, "What's the worst thing that could happen if you blow the opening line of your presentation during speech class? Will the class walk out? Throw things at you? If they laugh—so what? Giving a speech is good practice. So you mess up a few sentences! What's the worst thing that can happen? Somebody might chuckle, maybe they'll tease you about it."

You can identify worry thoughts because they usually start with a "What if . . . ," as in: "What if I walk into the party and I don't know anyone to talk to? What if I go to the dance and everyone there is wearing fancy dresses and my dress isn't right?"

Such "what if" questions were a problem for 16-year-old Debbie, whose life was ruled by "what-ifs." As noon approached, she'd think to herself, "What if there's no one to sit with at lunch? What if I don't have enough money for lunch and I come up short?" She was uncomfortable about going on a trip to the city with her aunt, worrying "What if I have to go to the bathroom? What if I have to order for myself at dinner?"

As Debbie discovered, worry thoughts often don't go away by themselves. They tend to replay over and over, until she expected the very worst that could possibly happen. In thinking about the upcoming trip, Debbie's worry thoughts got so bad she tried to get out of going. "What if I have to talk to the waiter in the restaurant? What if I say the wrong thing? What if I make a mistake? What if the waiter laughs at me?" Eventually, she became so overwrought that she told herself, "I can't go. It's too scary. I'll mess up and embarrass myself, and my aunt will think I'm a loser."

Typically, such self-talk goes round and round, making anxiety worse with each "what if," supporting the teen's pattern of avoidance. Therapists can help you look at these thoughts closely and identify the errors. For example, Debbie's therapist helped her see that it wasn't very likely that she'd make a mistake when she ordered her meal. After all, she'd ordered lots of meals with her parents.

Next, her therapist helped her work on coping techniques in case she did make a mistake and taught her how to replace her worry thoughts with calm, reassuring ones in the restaurant. "What would I say to a friend in this situation?" Debbie asked herself. The therapist pointed out that the waiter's job is to help her have a good dining experience and that his tip depends on making her feel comfortable. A waiter really isn't lurking about her table ready to laugh if she makes a simple mistake while ordering.

The "behavioral" aspect of therapy gradually exposes you to the circumstances that can trigger your panic. The central component of this treatment is exposure therapy, which involves helping patients gradually become more comfortable with situations that frighten them. First, your therapist may introduce you to the feared situation and then teach you techniques to cope. You might be asked to imagine your worst fear and then be encouraged to develop healthier responses. Lots of times you might find that group therapy can be a good way to work on this problem.

Your therapist also may try behavioral rehearsal, in which the two of you might role-play certain situations, trying out new behaviors ahead of time. This can make it much easier to practice these new behaviors before you're faced with real situations.

Cognitive-behavior therapy for social phobia also includes anxiety management training, which means you'll learn techniques to control your anxiety. Your therapist will teach you techniques that you can use to focus on the reality of what's happening now, rather than anticipating imaginary problems such as "What if I throw up in public?"

You'll also learn to stop fighting your fear. Instead, you'll be taught to expect it and accept it. You'll be taught how to focus on relaxation techniques that you can control, such as paying attention to your breathing, counting backwards from 100 by twos, or repeating an encouraging phrase: "What doesn't kill me makes me stronger" or "What's the worst that can happen?" Some kids find it helpful to imagine themselves relaxing at the beach or sitting on the top of a mountain. Some find it helpful to rub their hand on a podium or chair.

Behavioral therapy homework assignments can include making presentations in a real-life environment. This is where group therapy can help; socializing in a supportive group with others who know exactly what you're going through can let you practice in a fairly painless setting. It can help to practice giving a speech in a small group using the techniques you learned.

If your therapist is well trained in these techniques, he or she will never force or challenge you to do anything you really aren't ready to do. The motivation to work on these problems must come directly from you.

Assertiveness training. What most people don't know is that assertiveness training is really also a form of behavioral therapy. It's based on the idea that you can't feel anxiety and relaxation at the same time. Assertiveness training teaches people with social phobia to behave the way they would if they didn't feel anxious. It's almost like acting—actually, it's exactly like acting, because you're pretending you're somebody else, somebody who handles social situations well.

During assertiveness training, the therapist will ask you to think of someone you know who has very good social skills and then imagine that you're that person. You and the therapist will role-play a situation, and you'll act the way you think your imaginary person would act. By acting as you would act if you weren't afraid, you interfere with the anxiety. Therefore, you learn how to handle a situation assertively, and by behaving assertively, you inhibit the anxiety. In that situation where you'd been afraid, because you're acting like someone who isn't afraid, you don't feel anxious.

At this point, it might be helpful to understand the difference between assertiveness, passiveness, and aggressive behavior. People with social anxiety or social phobia can either be passive or aggressive—a doormat or steamroller. To be passive is sort of like being a doormat. If you're a passive person, you defer your own needs so that other people's needs always come first, before your own. If you're aggressive, you're more like a steamroller, and you do whatever it takes to get your own needs met, without any consideration for other people's needs. Assertiveness is a delicate balance between the two that lets you get your own needs met without violating the needs of others. Assertiveness training is designed to help you accomplish this.

Social skills training. Learning how to act in social situations is vital for people with social phobia or social anxiety. Because of their social anxiety, many people never get to the point that they know what to say in social situations. They don't know how to carry on a conversation or how to express interest in other people. They don't know what to say when given a compliment or how to act when they're criticized. Some people with social anxiety appear excessively needy or clingy, because their poor social skills make them desperate. Others seem aloof or distant, because their lack of social skill makes it hard for them to know how to communicate effectively.

Social skills training is nothing more than learning what to say in different situations and how to say it. Assertiveness training is dealing with the anxiety in social situations; social skills training is focused on providing the tools you need in social situations.

Many times people don't learn social skills during childhood—but it is possible to learn the knack of how to talk to people. Some kids know they don't have good skills. They know they're the only one not talking to other people at a party. A kid with social skills problems would be the person who latches on to just one other person. On the other hand, a person with social skills problems who tends to be more on the aggressive side, might walk all over other people and call it "their problem."

Rob was a 16-year-old high school junior who was very motivated to conquer his social phobia with some social skills training. He was so nervous and worried about being around other people that he had trouble making himself go to school. Social gatherings—parties and get-togethers—were the worst for him, because he always felt as if everyone was judging him. He didn't mind big groups, where he could slouch down in his chair and feel invisible.

But in smaller groups, Rob felt as if a big spotlight was shining right on his forehead. He just knew he was going to do or say something stupid, and everyone would laugh. Someone might ask him a question or expect him to be involved. He had particular problems in social situations where there wasn't much structure or rules he could follow for guidance. In such a group, he'd be very anxious and feel suffocated. He'd have trouble breathing, feeling flushed and dizzy. His chest would tighten, his heart would pound, and he would feel overwhelmed and "closed in."

Because he worried that if he went anywhere he'd feel anxious, and if he didn't go anywhere he wouldn't get anxious, he had a pretty big incentive for not going places. Instead, he'd huddle at home in his room and spend hours on the computer—one of the few times during his day that he felt completely relaxed. On his computer, he felt safe; because the computer wasn't evaluating him, it wasn't nearly as scary as interacting with other people.

During his first office visit, Rob learned some relaxation and breathing techniques. Rob claimed he just wasn't very good at visualization and imagining things, so instead of imagery he was taught deep muscle relaxation.

Rob listed a series of situations from least to most stressful to start working on reducing his level of panic, including situations at school, social settings, a small party where he knew people, a situation in which he was the center of attention, to the most stressful: walking into a party where he didn't know anyone and where there was the greatest number of unknowns.

By using relaxation techniques and breathing control, Rob began to practice handling social situations. Over a period of a few months, he went to more concerts, parties, and get-togethers. Soon he was doing better than ever in school, and he was much more involved in his community. Eventually, he was able to start going to new places and meeting new people, doing new things with new people in new places.

Let's get started. No matter what anxiety disorder you have, it's important to find a therapist who is well trained in cognitive-behavioral therapy. If you have a social phobia, it's also important that you locate a therapist who has worked with many teens who have this problem. You can get a referral from your doctor or contact the Anxiety Disorders Association of America or the Association for Behavioral and Cognitive Therapies. (You'll find contact information for all these groups in Appendix 1 at the back of the book).

When you go to your first session with the therapist, he or she should explain the techniques and strategies that will be used to help you conquer your social phobia. The therapist will probably then talk to you a bit about your interests and hobbies and will begin to ask you about the situations that seem to trigger your anxiety. Most therapists will begin teaching you methods to change your thoughts to help you develop new thinking skills and antianxiety strategies. Eventually, these new ways of thinking will become automatic. Then, once you start feeling a little more confident, the therapist can begin to help you change some of your behaviors. As you make headway, your therapist will probably suggest that you consider group therapy to work further on your anxieties.

Medications. Some teenagers need a bit of extra help while learning how to deal with their social anxieties; medication can help

Don't Force Yourself

Some of your well-meaning friends may try to push you into social situations that you fear, on the theory that flooding yourself with anxiety will somehow get rid of your social phobia. That just doesn't work for people in your situation.

In fact, trying to perform an activity that triggers a lot of anxiety will almost guarantee failure, which will lead to even more embarrassment and humiliation.

these individuals get the anxiety under control. Once medication calms your nerves and boosts your mood, you should get enough relief from your symptoms that you can practice the cognitive behavioral therapy techniques you learned. Drugs can reduce the tensions associated with entering the fearful situation, bring a racing heart and sweaty palms under control, and reduce some shyness. They won't cure your social phobia, but they can make your problem more manageable as you work on a solution.

Several types of drugs can be prescribed, either alone or in combination. The selective serotonin reuptake inhibitors (SSRIs) are a popular first choice, since they have fewer side effects and are in general considered safe. Paxil (paroxetine hydrochloride) was the first drug approved by the U.S. Food and Drug Administration specifically for treating social phobia. However, it's not officially approved for performance anxiety or shyness that falls short of being diagnosed as social phobia. In 2003 sertraline (Zoloft) was approved for short- and long-term (20-week) treatment of social phobia, and venlafaxine (Effexor), a serotonin/norepinephrine reuptake inhibitor, was also approved for the treatment of social phobia. Studies suggest that other SSRIs, such as fluoxetine (Prozac) or fluvoxamine (Luvox) also may be effective.

Doctors sometimes prescribe other drugs, such as beta blockers and benzodiazepines, to try to control the anxiety symptoms associated with social phobia. While these drugs have not been approved by the FDA specifically for treating social phobia, doctors can legally prescribe them if they believe a patient will benefit. Beta blockers used to treat social phobia include propranolol (Inderal) and atenolol (Tenormin). (Kids with asthma can't use beta blockers, however, because they can trigger an attack.) High-potency benzodiazepines, like clonazepam (Klonopin) and alprazolam (Xanax), also may be effective, although they have a more risky safety profile along with the danger of addiction. For some teens, the doctor may suggest a combination of a beta blocker and a low-dose clonazepam or alprazolam.

Some studies also suggest that a monoamine oxidase inhibitor (MAOI) such as phenelzine is effective in treating social phobias, but the dietary restrictions you have to follow with this drug make it an unpopular choice with teens. Occasionally, however, a person taking this drug will become too outgoing and talkative, which requires a dosage adjustment.

Many experts suggest that the best way to treat social fears is to begin by taking medication only when needed—for example, right before a specific stressful event that normally would trigger symptoms. If you have mostly physical symptoms, such as sweating or a pounding heart right before giving a speech, you'd take propranolol or atenolol about an hour before you had to mount the podium. (Propranolol seems to work better for situations that crop up only once in a while, while atenolol may work better for more constant social anxieties.)

However, if your symptoms are more in your head—in other words, you primarily worry about whether you'll mess up or whether others are judging you—you can take alprazolam an hour before the event. If, like many teens, you have a combination of both physical and mental symptoms, taking several medications may be your best bet. No matter which drugs you take, the benefits should last about four hours.

However, some teens never know when they might have an attack of social anxiety. If your symptoms appear not just at obvious times (such as right before you have to perform on stage) but at random times throughout the day or more constantly, you may need to take your medication on a daily basis.

OUTLOOK

If you get the right treatment for social phobia, you can eventually free yourself from the worries that have probably bothered you for so long. Remember that it takes time to get better. The improvements may seem small at first. Perhaps you'll be able to ask one question in class. But that's a big step in the right direction.

WHAT YOU NEED TO KNOW

▶ A true social phobia is much more than just normal shyness, simple "butterflies," or awkward feelings; it's extreme shyness accompanied by anxiety that interferes with your life and makes you avoid doing things you might otherwise like to do.

▶ Teens with social phobia have a persistent, intense, and chronic fear of being watched and judged by others and being embarrassed or humiliated by their own actions. Their fear may be so severe that it interferes with class or after-school activities.

▶ Social phobia may be limited to only one type of situation (such as a fear of eating, drinking, or writing in front of others), be centered around speaking or performing in public, or—in its most severe form—be so generalized that symptoms occur almost any time in public.

➤ The one symptom that everyone with social phobia has in common is that they know their fear is irrational.

➤ A few teens are so terribly shy or fearful about talking to others that they refuse to speak at all in class, to certain people, or in certain social situations, which is called selective mutism.

➤ Social anxiety and social phobia is probably related to some combination of brain function, heredity, learned behaviors, and personality.

➤ Social phobia often occurs along with another anxiety disorder, depression, or substance abuse.

➤ Social phobia almost always can be treated successfully with carefully targeted cognitive-behavioral therapy, assertiveness training, and social skills training. In severe cases, medications may be required.

5

"I Just Can't Stop!": Obsessive-Compulsive Disorder (OCD)

Charles was a 13-year-old middle school student referred for treatment after being hospitalized several times. As he entered adolescence, his normal fastidiousness began to take on a whole new dimension as he became obsessed with keeping his room neat. Soon he also became convinced that someone might break into his home, which forced him to check constantly that the front and back doors were locked. No sooner did he try the doors to confirm they were fastened than he had to go back and recheck the locks "just to make sure."

These concerns gradually worsened until he also became worried about being contaminated with germs. His fears of contamination grew to the point where he was unable to use toilet paper for fear he would inadvertently touch his feces, so instead of using toilet paper he used towels and clothing to wipe himself. Unwilling to let his mom know what he was doing, he hid the soiled items in closets, under the bed, and behind his cabinets because he was so ashamed.

Things finally came to a head when his mother discovered his stash of soiled laundry and confronted Charles. Breaking down, he told how his life had begun to revolve around keeping his room spotless, the doors locked, and his body germ free. Alarmed, his mother immediately made an appointment with a psychiatrist, who prescribed medication, and with a psychologist for therapy. After extensive cognitive-behavioral treatment, Charles made significant progress. He began using toilet paper again, was able to resume playing sports, and reduced his abnormal checking.

Everyone occasionally obsesses about some minor issue ("Did I turn off the iron? Did I lock the front door?"). However, if you have obsessive-compulsive disorder (OCD), your ritual behaviors may literally take over your life. People with OCD are plagued by persistent, recurring thoughts called *obsessions,* which reflect exaggerated anxiety or fears such as being contaminated or behaving improperly. The obsessions may lead the person to perform rituals or routines called *compulsions,* such as washing hands, repeating phrases, or hoarding. This relieves the anxiety caused by the obsession.

Most teens with obsessive-compulsive disorder know the rituals and compulsions don't make sense. Although they're usually deeply ashamed of these behaviors, they can't overcome them without treatment.

OCD is a fairly common problem that affects about equal numbers of boys and girls and usually first appears during adolescence or early adulthood. In the United States, about 1 million children and teens have OCD. But sometimes kids feel ashamed about the worries and the rituals they perform to protect against bad things. They know their behavior seems silly to other people, so they often keep it to themselves. Most teens with OCD don't talk about it. You could know someone who has OCD and not even realize it.

If you have OCD, then you know that living with it can be very hard. Compulsions often take up a great deal of your time and energy, making it hard to finish homework, do chores, or have any fun. Some kids find it hard to go to school or make friends. But dealing with something so tough all alone can make it even harder.

Your friends and family love you, but they may have a hard time understanding what you're going through. They may think it's just a bad habit. They don't understand that the need to do rituals can feel too strong to ignore. Some kids say that OCD feels like a constant voice inside their head telling them bad things could happen and making them do certain things so that no matter how much they want to stop, they can't. It may feel as if OCD is running your life.

SYMPTOMS

Obsessive-compulsive disorder, or OCD, involves anxious thoughts or rituals you feel you can't control and that intrude when you're trying to think of or do other things. Some teens have symptoms that come and go, some get better over time, and others grow progressively worse.

Obsessions. It's normal for kids to worry once in a while about things that probably will never happen, such as kidnapping, fires, or earthquakes. This kind of worry is actually helpful, because it can help you learn how to keep yourself safe. Normal worries like these may pop into your head and then you forget about them; they do not cause too much of a problem. OCD is much more than this type of normal worry. Instead, kids with OCD worry in an intense, almost nonstop way. In fact, the worries are so constant that it's hard to think of anything else; your brain just replays them over and over, making you feel worse and worse. It's kind of like when you get a song stuck in your head—no matter how much you try to ignore it, your brain just keeps playing it back. You may even make up rules to follow that help control the anxiety you feel when having obsessive thoughts.

Having unending worrying thoughts that you can't stop can feel scary and upsetting. These intrusive thoughts can make it hard to concentrate on anything else, so your schoolwork might suffer. OCD can take the fun out of almost anything.

Compulsions. In addition to these persistent, unwelcome thoughts or images, if you have OCD you also may have an urgent need to engage in certain rituals, such as constantly washing your hands, lining up your shoes, or checking and rechecking that the windows are closed. When you perform these rituals, your anxiety may fade away, but not for long. Soon your discomfort returns, and you feel the urge to repeat your behaviors. These rituals or compulsions may have blended into your daily routine, and they may not be directly related to the obsessive thought. For example, Harry has intrusive, aggressive thoughts about his sister—but he compulsively counts ceiling tiles in an effort to control those thoughts.

Common Obsessions

> dirt, germs, or contamination

> order, symmetry, exactness

> certain sounds, images, words, or numbers

> harming a family member or friend

> "evil" thoughts

Many kids who don't have OCD may be superstitious or have rituals they perform sometimes. Maybe you bring your lucky pen to school for a test or say a certain poem every time before you run onto the court for your basketball game. Perhaps you have a lucky rabbit's foot or still like to sleep with a battered old stuffed animal from when you were a kid.

But compulsions are much more than performing a ritual for luck. Kids with OCD feel they have to do certain things over and over to keep safe. They think that doing a certain ritual will make a bad feeling go away, and they feel scared that if they don't do the ritual just exactly right, something bad will happen. They don't get any pleasure from their rituals, which just provide temporary relief from the anxiety that grows stronger for every second they don't perform them.

Teens with OCD worry a lot and feel scared about bad things that could happen. Some teens, like Charles, are afraid of getting dirty or catching germs, so they wash their hands over and over. Others always worry that someone they love will get sick or die, and some teens may have frequent thoughts of violence and worry that they will hurt people they love. Some kids are filled with doubt and feel they need to check things repeatedly. They figure that if they can just make everything around them exactly right or extremely neat all the time, they can keep bad things from happening. Others may spend long periods touching things or counting. They may be preoccupied by order or symmetry or have persistent thoughts of performing sexual acts that are repugnant to them. Still others are troubled by thoughts that are against their religious beliefs. Some teens worry about thinking bad thoughts, worrying that just thinking about something bad could make it come true.

Almost everybody can identify with some of the symptoms of OCD, such as checking the stove repeatedly to make sure it's off before leaving the house. But if you have OCD, such activities consume at least an hour a day, are very distressing, and interfere with daily life. Some teenagers with OCD worry so much that they can spend the whole day worrying and trying to make sure the bad things they worry about don't happen. If OCD gets serious enough, it can keep you from doing well in school (it's hard to concentrate when you're busy with compulsions and obsessions) or carrying out normal chores around the house.

JUST COMPULSIVE—OR IS IT OCD?

Some teenagers are perfectionists. They work very hard in school to make sure they get all A's. Kate had to make sure that each paper she completed was perfect. Brittany got upset if every math problem she completed wasn't lined up neatly on the page. Sam always tried to hand in his reports three days early. Molly practiced shooting baskets for hours on end, and Steve vacuumed the rug in his bedroom every night. The history teacher told the class that each person had to complete 25 notecards; Cimmie handed in 345. All this may seem a bit compulsive, but that doesn't mean these kids have obsessive-compulsive disorder.

There's a difference between being a compulsive perfectionist and having OCD. Lots of teenagers belong to a group of people who

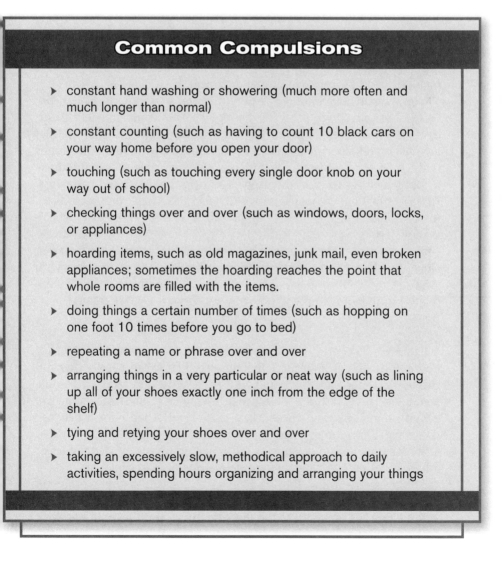

Common Compulsions

- constant hand washing or showering (much more often and much longer than normal)

- constant counting (such as having to count 10 black cars on your way home before you open your door)

- touching (such as touching every single door knob on your way out of school)

- checking things over and over (such as windows, doors, locks, or appliances)

- hoarding items, such as old magazines, junk mail, even broken appliances; sometimes the hoarding reaches the point that whole rooms are filled with the items.

- doing things a certain number of times (such as hopping on one foot 10 times before you go to bed)

- repeating a name or phrase over and over

- arranging things in a very particular or neat way (such as lining up all of your shoes exactly one inch from the edge of the shelf)

- tying and retying your shoes over and over

- taking an excessively slow, methodical approach to daily activities, spending hours organizing and arranging your things could be called compulsive. That means they hold themselves to a very high standard in everything they do so they can feel successful. This is NOT obsessive-compulsive disorder. Behaviors associated with obsessive-compulsive disorder *interfere with everyday functioning.* A kid with OCD doesn't just line up math problems neatly; he lines up items in his room, over and over, for hours at a time. It's hard for him to get anything else done, because all his time is spent lining up items.

COEXISTING CONDITIONS

Just as with other anxiety disorders, if you have OCD you also may have other mental health issues. Some teens with OCD also have depression (but otherwise, having OCD doesn't mean you are generally sad or unhappy). And teens who are just depressed almost never have the kind of intrusive thoughts typical of OCD.

Some teens have another anxiety disorder in addition to OCD, but OCD is usually pretty easy to distinguish from other anxiety disorders. For example, OCD and post-traumatic stress disorder (PTSD) are easy to tell apart, since OCD is not caused by trauma. Some teens with OCD also have eating disorders. Others try unsuccessfully to use alcohol or drugs to calm themselves or stop the unwanted behaviors. About 20 percent of people with OCD also have tics, such as sudden, uncontrollable physical movements (such as eye blinking) or vocalizations (such as throat clearing).

If you already have a learning disorder, OCD can make it worse or cause problems with attention and concentration. It can interfere with your ability to learn at school. Most of the time, these behaviors are related to the OCD and will go away when your OCD is treated.

CAUSE

You can't catch OCD from someone else, like a bad case of the flu. Other than that, scientists don't know exactly how and why some teenagers get OCD. But it's clear that having OCD isn't your fault. You haven't done anything wrong, and you're not a bad person because you have this problem. Nor is OCD caused by family problems or attitudes in your family, such as too much emphasis on cleanliness or a belief that certain thoughts are dangerous or unacceptable.

Some experts think the problem is biological—a brain problem. Some think it could be inherited in some cases or might occur after an infection. Others believe the disorder stems from learned behavior or a combination of brain problems and learned behavior.

Faulty wiring. OCD is a type of anxiety that happens when there's a problem with the way your brain handles normal worry thoughts and doubts. There is more and more evidence that OCD is caused by abnormal functioning of brain circuitry, especially in parts of the brain called the basal ganglia and striatum. Research suggests that OCD might have something to do with the chemicals that carry messages to nerve cells in the brain. If these chemicals are blocked or if there aren't enough of them in the brain, messages about doubt and worry seem to get stuck, replaying in the brain over and over. Specifically, a low level of serotonin, one of those chemical messengers, may contribute to obsessive-compulsive disorder.

Brain scan studies using a technique called positron emission tomography (PET) have compared the brains of people with and without OCD. Those with OCD have different patterns of brain activity than people with other mental illnesses or people with no mental problems. PET scans also show that in people with OCD, both behavioral therapy and medication trigger changes in the striatum. This is strong evidence that both psychotherapy and medication affect the brain. These scans also show that people with OCD use different brain circuitry when thinking than do people without the disorder.

Heredity. Scientists think that at least in some cases, OCD might be inherited, because lots of teens with OCD have someone else in their family with OCD or another type of anxiety. Government scientists have found several mutations in a gene (the human serotonin transporter gene, hSERT) that seem to be linked to OCD. Exactly how this happens, however, isn't clear. Scientists also think that mutant gene effects probably combine with stress to trigger OCD. Scientists are trying to learn more about these genes that might make people more sensitive to worrying.

It's also possible to inherit a tendency to react strongly to stress. This stronger-than-normal reaction may trigger the intrusive thoughts and rituals of OCD.

Strep infections. In rare cases, OCD may be triggered by the way your body responds to a strep infection. Of course, many people may carry the bacteria that cause strep throat, and they don't have any symptoms of mental illness. But some research suggests that occasionally a strep infection is followed by the sudden appearance of very intense OCD symptoms. When scientists compared children diagnosed with OCD and some tic conditions with healthy kids, they found that children with one of the disorders were twice as likely to have had a strep infection within three months of diagnosis.

The association between these disorders and strep was given the initials PANDAS, which stands for pediatric autoimmune neuropsychiatric disorders associated with streptococcal infection. But the link is still considered controversial. In research published in the July 2005 issue of *Pediatrics,* scientists studied medical records for 144 children diagnosed with OCD, Tourette syndrome, or a separate tic disorder and compared their records with those of a larger group of children without the conditions. It turned out that children with one of the neurological disorders were twice as likely to have had a strep infection in the three months before diagnosis. The association was even stronger for kids who had more than one strep infection.

Not all experts accept this link, but those who do suggest that OCD might be triggered by antibodies produced during a strep infection. Antibodies are proteins the body produces to fight infection. In certain areas of the brain more antibodies are present in people with OCD.

Of course, teens usually don't develop OCD when they get strep infections, and only a small percentage of kids with OCD have had strep infections.

TREATMENT

OCD generally responds well to treatment with carefully tailored psychotherapy, but sometimes some kids also need medication. In at least one national study, a combination of therapy and medication worked better in treating OCD than either treatment alone. The National Institute of Mental Health recommends that treatment begin with cognitive-behavioral therapy (CBT), either alone or with a selective serotonin reuptake inhibitor (SSRI) antidepressant. Talk to your doctor and therapist about what combination they think might be best for you.

Psychotherapy. Special "talk therapy" is the best treatment for OCD. Called cognitive-behavioral therapy (CBT), this type of counseling can help you recognize, understand, and restructure your distorted thoughts into fact-based ones. In this kind of treatment, you learn how to retrain your thoughts and routines so that compulsive behaviors are no longer necessary. It can help you learn to deal with anxiety, face your fears, and resist compulsions. Gradually, this kind of therapy should help you handle OCD.

CBT was effective in helping 15-year-old Dennis, who had a variety of problems related to his OCD: checking, fear of contamination by germs, and a need to have everything in its place. Very rigid in his beliefs about what was right and wrong, Dennis also felt that he was intrinsically flawed and that if he didn't perform all of his OCD behaviors, something bad would happen and it would be his fault. If he didn't check the doors exactly three times to make sure they were locked, somebody would break in and burglarize his house. If he didn't clean, he'd get sick from germs and might die. He had to keep his room spotless with constant cleaning, because if there was a piece of paper on the floor people might trip on it and hurt themselves.

In Dennis's world, everything had its place. If his mother moved so much as a paperback on his nightstand, he would know and put it back the way it had been. Then he'd have to completely clean the entire room again to make sure everything was in its proper place. He worried that someone might trip over something even as small as a paper clip. His days were spent redoing and recleaning and reorganizing things constantly, to the point that he had no time for anything else.

As many people with OCD do, he knew that his behavior wasn't normal and that his compulsions didn't make sense, but he felt compelled to do them and couldn't stop himself.

During our first session, we evaluated his automatic thought that something bad might happen if he didn't carry out his behaviors. Some of the questions we asked included

> ▶ "What's the worst that could happen if you didn't check or clean?"
> ▶ "If somebody stepped on a piece of paper on the floor, how bad would that be?
> ▶ "What's the likelihood someone would trip and get hurt?"
> ▶ "What's the chance that you'll get sick from germs and die?"

Although Dennis understood that his automatic thoughts didn't make sense, his anxiety was still high. It took almost a year and a half to work through his issues, along with medication, for Dennis to overcome the most severe of his OCD behavior. At home, Dennis would be asked to perform various experiments, such as intentionally leaving something out of place in his room, which was very difficult for him. He would say that he was afraid that if he knowingly left a paper clip on the floor it meant he was intentionally trying to hurt somebody. After this experiment, I'd ask; "When nobody got hurt, what do you think that means?" After one or two times of leaving a paper clip on the floor, he'd say, "We've just been lucky that no one got hurt." We had to keep doing the same experiment, over and over. Paper clip on the floor—no injury.

It was the same with his checking behavior. He practiced not checking, and eventually he got to the point that he didn't check and nobody was hurt. These endless homework assignments were a way of proving that his fears and thoughts were groundless—there wasn't a direct connection between safety, checking, and being neat.

As a result, Dennis decreased the amount of time he spent checking. He still preferred to have things in an orderly way, but he didn't have to perform his rituals (when he was putting things in place, he would always recite a jingle to himself over and over in an obsessive way) while he'd clean. He still didn't like touching sticky substances, but he could tolerate brief exposure without fear of getting a disease.

Exposure. This strategy is an important part of CBT therapy for obsessive-compulsive disorder. It's based on the idea that anxiety usually lessens after you've been in contact with something you fear for a period of time. Therefore, if you've got an obsession about germs, you might be asked to touch something you consider germy (such as a handful of dollar bills) until your anxiety is extinguished. Or maybe you would be asked to wait five minutes after you've gotten your hands dirty before washing them. Your anxiety will decrease after you keep exposing yourself to the germs, until you no longer fear the contact.

Response prevention. Exposure works best if it's combined with response prevention. In this approach, you're voluntarily exposed to whatever triggers your obsessive thoughts; then the therapist teaches you techniques to handle it and deal with your anxiety rather than perform the compulsive rituals. If you're uncomfortable about germs, you might be asked to handle the dollar bills and then not conduct your washing ritual. As treatment progresses and you practice the techniques, your symptoms gradually get less intense and less frequent.

In general, exposure is the best technique for decreasing anxiety and obsessions, while response prevention is more helpful in decreasing compulsive behaviors. It may sound difficult, but you'd be surprised how many teenagers, even those who have wrestled with OCD for several years, have few problems tolerating exposure and response prevention once they get started.

Dennis also worked on exposure and response prevention to deal with his fear of contamination. He had the most trouble with things that were sticky, such as jelly or glue. During our session, we would place a sticky substance on his hand and then he would practice relaxation and breathing as he dealt with his anxiety. Eventually, he learned that having a sticky substance on his hands wasn't dangerous and that he wouldn't get sick.

Cognitive therapy. The first few times you work with exposure and response therapy might be hard. As you practice, your therapist will probably add some cognitive therapy strategies to help you handle your anxiety, catastrophic thinking, and responsibility fears. For example, Sean worried that if he didn't remind his mother to lock the door, she'd die, because a burglar would break in and kill her. Cognitive therapy helped Sean with these feelings and his sense of responsibility by helping him evaluate the assumptions in his obsession. By using this type of thought control, Sean is better able to work on his exposure and response therapy because he doesn't have to keep calling home to check.

Your therapist may have some other tricks to share with you as well. One technique is to listen for a long period to a spoken description of an obsession on a closed-loop audiotape (a technique called *satiation*).

You might have success with *habit reversal,* in which an OCD ritual is replaced with a different non-OCD behavior. With habit reversal, you're trying to replace the harmful behavior with another harmless behavior. At first, you'll need to be able to become aware of your OCD behavior. Your therapist may ask you to write down when, where, and under what circumstances you experience your symptom. If repeatedly washing your hands is one of your OCD symptoms, a competing response would be to clench your fist (since you can't wash if you're clenching). Another important part of habit reversal training is practicing meditation, abdominal breathing, or progressive muscle relaxation. Other teens find it helpful to receive rewards as incentives for doing the new behavior.

Let's get started . . . It's important to find a therapist who is well trained in cognitive behavior therapy. You can get a referral from your doctor or check with the Academy of Cognitive Therapy, Obsessive Compulsive Foundation, which has a list of well-trained treatment providers who belong to the organization. You could also contact the Anxiety Disorders Association of America or the Association for Behavioral and Cognitive Therapies. You'll find contact information for all these groups in Appendix 1 at the back of this book.

When you go to your first session with the therapist, he or she will probably start by talking to you a bit about your interests and hobbies and about what your life is like. The therapist will also ask you about your compulsions or obsessions. Then you'll start to learn some different ways to deal with your worries so that you don't have to perform a ritual. At first, treatment will be aimed at ending the current episode of OCD using the strategies described above. Once that's under control, your therapist will shift his or her attention to keeping symptoms from coming back, or *maintenance therapy.*

At first it will probably seem hard to stop performing rituals, but a therapist can teach a teen how to feel safe enough to try little by little. It's tough at first, but those who stick with it begin to feel stronger and braver in overcoming OCD. Once they learn ways to get their worries under control, they start to practice them. As with anything new (such as playing the piano or doing a layup), the more they practice, the better they can do it. When kids practice what they learn in behavior therapy, they find out it actually works. It's a great relief when the symptoms of OCD weaken and the kids begin to feel stronger.

Kids with OCD usually go to therapy about once or twice a week at first to develop a CBT treatment plan and to monitor symptoms, medication doses, and side effects. They'll also usually be given daily exposure and response prevention homework. It may seem inconvenient, but homework is necessary because the situations or objects that trigger OCD are unique and probably can't be duplicated in your therapist's office.

Intensive CBT, which involves two to three hours of therapist-assisted exposure and response prevention daily for three weeks, is the fastest treatment for OCD. Sometimes your therapist may have to come to your house for treatment if you're having some very stubborn symptoms, or you may need to be admitted to a hospital for a brief time.

As you get better, you'll see your therapist less often. Once you're better, you might see your therapist just once a year. Getting better can take anywhere from a few months to a few years.

Medications. Medications can ease the intensity of your intrusive thoughts and compulsions and can quiet down some of your worries and fears, but they can't stop them from occurring in the first place. What medications can do is to weaken the worries so that you can use various self-help skills to control them. These medications help boost the level of certain brain chemicals and help them work properly, which can improve some cases of OCD.

Currently, six medications called selective serotonin reuptake inhibitors (SSRIs) can help in treating OCD. They work by boosting the brain levels of serotonin, a chemical that is used to send and receive messages in your brain, and enhancing your brain's ability to use this chemical. Doctors believe that serotonin plays a crucial role in OCD, depression, and other mood problems. The six SSRIs prescribed for OCD are

- ➤ citalopram (Celexa)
- ➤ escitalopram (Lexapro)
- ➤ fluoxetine (Prozac)
- ➤ fluvoxamine (Luvox)
- ➤ paroxetine (Paxil)
- ➤ sertraline (Zoloft)

It may take between five and 10 weeks before the medication begins to work. All of these SSRIs are about equally effective, but they typically have slightly different side effects. Your doctor will know the best drug for your own special symptom profile and history of medication reactions. Most patients notice some benefit after three or four weeks, but the maximum benefit won't be evident until about 10 or 12 weeks at the right dose. If it's clear that a medication isn't working as well as it should, however, your doctor will probably recommend switching to another SSRI. Since some teens do better on one than another, it's important to keep trying until your doctor finds the medication and dosage schedule that's best for you. Before deciding that a treatment has failed, your therapist needs to be sure that the treatment has been given in a large enough dose for long enough.

The antidepressant clomipramine (Anafranil) also helps ease the strength of obsessions, but this drug has a more complicated set of side effects than the SSRIs. Imipramine and alprazolam and the mild

If You Get Frustrated with Medication

If you feel that your medication isn't working or it's causing side effects, tell your doctor. *Don't quit taking the medicine on your own.* It's harder to get your symptoms under control than to keep them under control, so you don't want to mess around with your medication on your own. You and your doctor can work together to find the best medicine for you.

tranquilizer buspirone (BuSpar) also may work for some teenagers. Some scientists have combined buspirone with clomipramine to successfully treat this problem. Teenagers with OCD who also have an underlying mood disorder may benefit from the drug lithium.

If you have tics as a part of your OCD symptoms, your doctor may suggest a combination of an SSRI and a neuroleptic such as risperidone (Risperdal).

Side effects. All the SSRIs have similar side effects, including nervousness, sleeplessness, restlessness, nausea, and diarrhea. More severe side effects are associated with larger doses and a rapid increase in the dose, which is why your doctor will start you at the lowest dose possible.

The most common side effects of clomipramine are dry mouth, sedation, dizziness, and weight gain. Because clomipramine is more likely to cause problems with blood pressure and irregular heartbeats, adolescents and anyone with heart problems must have electrocardiograms before beginning treatment with this drug.

Over time, your body will probably begin to tolerate the SSRIs, unlike clomipramine. However, all SSRIs should be tapered and stopped slowly to lessen the chance of the return of symptoms and withdrawal reactions.

FAMILY SUPPORT

Just like any chronic illness, OCD can take a toll on your family life too. Household routines may be disrupted, and sometimes family members must make special plans or allowances for your problem. Sometimes teens with OCD are reluctant to participate in family activities as they have in the past. All of this can interfere with having a happy, healthy family.

Family problems don't cause OCD, but the way your family reacts to your symptoms can affect the disorder. This is why it's so important for every member of your family to learn as much as they can about OCD, so they know what to expect and better understand the recovery process. In family therapy, the whole family goes to see your therapist to learn more about the problem. The therapist can help your family learn how to avoid getting pulled into your rituals and how to understand that negative comments or criticism often make OCD worse. A calm, supportive family can help improve your situation.

You may want to check out teen support groups too. Sharing your worries and experiences with others who've experienced the same thing can be a terrific boost. If you're like many teens, you probably hide your OCD symptoms from your friends. Joining a support group is a good way to feel less isolated and alone and to learn new tips for coping with OCD. (See Appendix 1 at the back of this book for associations and support groups.)

It will be much easier for you to get better if you have your family's support, although there's no magic cure. Getting better takes hard work, and the more support you have, the better.

MAINTENANCE THERAPY

Once your OCD symptoms are eliminated or reduced, you'll begin the maintenance portion of your treatment. Most experts recommend that you visit your therapist once a month for at least six months but ideally continue these monthly visits for at least a year before trying to stop medications or the CBT. This is because relapse is very common when a medication is stopped.

If your OCD keeps returning, you may need to continue your medication for a very long time—even for the rest of your life. Typically, this is recommended if you have had two to four severe relapses (or three or four milder relapses) after an initial successful treatment.

However, if you've done well with your maintenance treatment and your doctor decides you don't need long-term medication, you can probably begin slowly decreasing your medication by 25 percent while having CBT booster sessions to prevent a relapse. After two months,

Call Your Therapist If You Have

► sudden recurrence of severe OCD symptoms

► worsening OCD symptoms that don't respond to your CBT strategies

► changes in medication side effects

► new symptoms of another disorder (such as depression or panic)

► any change that you think might worsen your OCD (such as going to a new school or your parents getting a divorce)

your doctor can then lower your medication again, depending on how you respond, continuing to taper the dose until you are no longer taking any medication.

OUTLOOK

If you get the right treatment for OCD, you can eventually free yourself from the worries and rituals that have probably bothered you for so long. Remember that it takes time to get better. The improvements may seem small at first. Maybe you'll just be able to decrease the time you spend washing your hands by 10 minutes a day. But that's a big step in the right direction.

Since OCD can come and go many times during your life, you and your family need to learn all about OCD and its treatment. It will take courage, hard work, and lots of practice. Plenty of kids with OCD have done it. If you have OCD, with the right help you can do it too.

WHAT YOU NEED TO KNOW

➤ Everyone occasionally obsesses about some minor issue, but if you have obsessive-compulsive disorder (OCD), your ritual behaviors may literally take over your life.

➤ OCD causes persistent, recurring thoughts called obsessions, which reflect exaggerated anxiety or fears, such as being contaminated or behaving improperly. The obsessions may lead to rituals or routines called compulsions, such as washing hands, repeating phrases, or hoarding, to relieve the anxiety caused by the obsession.

➤ Most teens with obsessive-compulsive disorder know that the rituals and compulsions don't make sense. Although they're usually deeply ashamed of these behaviors, they can't overcome them without treatment.

➤ OCD affects about a million boys and girls, usually first appearing during adolescence or early adulthood.

➤ Kids with OCD worry in an intense, almost nonstop way and have difficulty thinking of anything else.

➤ Typical OCD obsessions include fears of dirt, germs, or contamination; a need for order, symmetry, and exactness; thoughts of certain sounds, images, words, or numbers; harming a family member or friend; or having evil thoughts.

➤ Kids with OCD don't perform a ritual for luck; they believe they have to do certain things over and over to keep safe or to make a bad feeling go away. They feel scared that if they don't perform the ritual exactly right, something bad will happen.

▸ Common compulsions include constant washing, cleaning, counting, touching, checking, hoarding, or arranging; doing things a certain number of times; repeating a word or phrase; tying and retying shoes; or taking an excessively slow, methodical approach to daily activities.

▸ There's a difference between being a compulsive perfectionist and having OCD: Behaviors associated with OCD interfere with everyday functioning.

▸ People with OCD also may have other mental health issues.

▸ Experts aren't sure what causes OCD, but it may be linked to a brain problem, learned behavior, or a combination of both; to heredity; or to an infection.

▸ OCD generally responds well to a combination of treatment with carefully tailored psychotherapy and medication.

▸ Cognitive-behavioral therapy is the best treatment for OCD, helping you recognize, understand, and restructure negative thoughts into more positive ones.

▸ Exposure is a strategy based on the idea that anxiety usually lessens after you've been in contact with something you fear for a time, so if you have an obsession about germs, you might be asked to touch something you consider germy (such as a handful of dollar bills).

▸ Exposure works best if it's combined with response prevention, in which you're voluntarily exposed to whatever triggers obsessions and then taught techniques to deal with your anxiety rather than perform the compulsive rituals.

▸ As you practice, your therapist may add some ways to help handle anxiety and fears by evaluating the assumptions in an obsession.

▸ Medications can ease the intensity of your intrusive thoughts and compulsions and can quiet down some of your worries and fears so you can use self-help skills to control them. Drugs can't stop these thoughts from occurring in the first place.

▸ Fluoxetine (Prozac), fluvoxamine (Luvox), sertraline (Zoloft), paroxetine (Paxil), and citalopram (Celexa) are used to treat OCD and may take from five to 10 weeks to work.

▸ If you have tics, your doctor may suggest a combination of an SSRI and neuroleptics.

▸ Family problems don't cause OCD, but family therapy can help the family learn how to avoid getting pulled into your rituals and how to understand that negative comments or criticism often make OCD worse.

➤ Once symptoms improve, you'll visit a therapist monthly for at least six months to a year before trying to stop medications or CBT.

➤ OCD can be successfully treated, but it can come and go many times during your life.

6

"The Memory Haunts Me!": Post-Traumatic Stress Disorder (PTSD)

Jim, 13, was riding in the back seat of the family car late one night on vacation in Boston. Suddenly, the air was filled with the screech of tires as the car collided with another in a busy intersection. Jim's father was driving, and he swears that the other car ran a red light. Although no one was hurt, this was the first accident Jim had ever experienced, and it terrified him. Ever since, Jim has been tormented by nightly car wreck nightmares, in which the car he's riding in is wrecked in some new method. Jim also feels on edge a lot, and—even worse—he's become paranoid about riding in a car with his father. He goes to great lengths to avoid having to sit in the same car with his father. Sudden noises send his heart racing, and unwanted images of the wreck keep popping into Jim's mind.

These images pop up even when he's concentrating on something else—and they're so scary that he's been finding it hard to concentrate at all. Things he used to like to do, such as listen to his iPod or play ball with his friends, just don't seem like much fun anymore.

Jim didn't realize it, but he was experiencing post-traumatic stress disorder (PTSD), a condition that occurs after someone experiences a traumatic, potentially life-threatening event, triggering frightening thoughts and memories and emotional numbness. Any teen exposed to a traumatic event can develop PTSD. Although most Americans first heard about PTSD when Vietnam War veterans were diagnosed with the problem, it's not just related to war. It can be caused by any number of traumatic events, such as a violent mugging or rape, being kidnapped or held captive, child abuse, serious car accidents, or natural disasters like floods or earthquakes. The event that triggers PTSD could be something that threatened your life or the life of someone close to you or something you saw, such as a plane crash.

Kids are often more easily traumatized than adults, which is why something that might not be too upsetting to an adult (such as a turbulent plane ride) might be very traumatic to a child. As a result, the child may reexperience the event through nightmares, through constant thoughts about what happened, or by reenacting the event while playing. Children with this pattern also can experience symptoms of general anxiety, such as having trouble sleeping and eating or being irritable. Many children exhibit other physical symptoms as well, such as being easily startled.

CAUSE

It's common for people to have very strong emotional reactions to traumatic situations. Understanding normal responses to these abnormal events can help you cope well with your feelings, thoughts, and behaviors.

The hippocampus is a part of the brain that helps encode information into memories and processes threatening or traumatic events. Studies have shown that the hippocampus seems to be smaller in people who have been abused or who have served in a war, which could explain why individuals with post-traumatic stress disorder have flashbacks, memory problems, and fragmented memories of the traumatic event.

Government-supported studies of twins and families suggest that genes also play a role in the origin of many anxiety disorders, such as PTSD. But heredity alone can't explain what goes awry; your traumatic experience also plays a part. In other words, trauma triggers the anxiety disorder, but genetic factors may explain why only certain people who were exposed to similar traumatic events develop full-blown PTSD. Researchers are trying to figure out how genetics and experience interact so they will be better able to prevent and treat PTSD.

Girls and young women are more likely than guys to develop PTSD.

SYMPTOMS

There are three main symptoms associated with PTSD:

- ▶ reliving the traumatic event in flashbacks or nightmares
- ▶ avoiding places or events related to the trauma
- ▶ feeling numb

These are the three basic symptoms, but teens may show different symptoms than adults do, and very young children may not show many symptoms at all because they can't describe what happened to them or how they feel about it. Instead, young children may report more general fears. For example, a young child who was caught in a tornado in her home may suddenly develop nightmares, a fear of strangers or of separation, or a preoccupation with certain words. Children might avoid situations that may or may not be related to the trauma. Because most kids can't cope effectively with sudden stress, they look to family members for comfort. Some children in this situation may repeat the trauma during play or may regress; for instance, they may stop being toilet trained or become inexplicably aggressive.

Elementary school–aged children may not experience visual flashbacks or amnesia, but they might obsess about omens or warnings and worry that they must pay close attention so they'll be able to recognize future warning signs. Older kids can have sleep or appetite problems, refuse to do chores, get in fights, withdraw from social activity, or seek extra attention. They might also complain about physical problems such as vague aches, headaches, or bowel problems.

By adolescence, however, teenagers can experience the classic adult symptoms of PTSD, yet they are also more likely than younger children or adults to become impulsive and aggressive. If you've experienced a traumatic event, you may notice that you get more headaches and tension or unexplained rashes or that you have problems with appetite and sleep. You may feel either agitated or apathetic.

Not surprisingly, children and adolescents who have experienced traumatic events often develop other problems as well, such as fear, anxiety, depression, self-destructive behavior, feelings of isolation, poor self-esteem, difficulty trusting others, and substance abuse. They may have trouble with friends and family and start to act out. Their schoolwork may suffer, and their grades may begin to slide.

No matter what the cause, many kids with PTSD relive the trauma over and over, either during nightmares or through flashbacks during the day, especially when they are exposed to events or objects that remind them of the traumatic episode. They may also have problems with sleep, or they may feel numb. Some are easily startled. Still others lose interest in things they used to enjoy, or they have trouble feeling affectionate with anyone. Some feel irritable, aggressive, or even violent.

If you have PTSD, anything that reminds you of the trauma can be so disturbing that you avoid certain places or situations that bring back those memories. Anniversaries of the traumatic event are often very difficult.

If you have a severe case of PTSD, you may have trouble paying attention in school or enjoying time with friends. For example, if you developed PTSD after living through a tornado, an unexpected clap of thunder could trigger a flashback or an intrusive memory. The flashback might include images, sounds, smells, or feelings—or you might lose touch with reality and think that the traumatic event is happening all over again.

Timeline. Not every traumatized person develops PTSD, but in those who do, symptoms typically begin within three months of the trauma and last for at least a month. Some kids with PTSD recover within six months, but others have symptoms that last much longer. In some cases, the condition may be chronic. Occasionally PTSD doesn't show up until many years after the traumatic event. The disorder is often accompanied by depression, substance abuse, or other anxiety disorders.

RISK FACTORS

Those who experience severe trauma or who are directly involved may be more likely to develop PTSD. The way your family members support one another and cope with the problem also can affect the severity of symptoms, since research shows that kids with the most family support and least parental distress have fewer symptoms.

The type of trauma also influences the likelihood of developing PTSD. Typically, symptoms are worse as a result of deliberate trauma; that's why incidences of rape and assault are more likely to cause PTSD than other events. For those unlucky enough to experience more than one traumatic event, the chance of developing PTSD increases. Other risk factors include having to cope with stress before the trauma occurred, parents' extreme response to the trauma, and a belief that you've been irreversibly damaged as a result of the event.

TREATMENT

Although PTSD improves with time in some lucky children and teens, most kids who aren't treated continue experiencing PTSD symptoms years after the event. That's why it's important to get treated as quickly as possible. But first, there are some things you can do to help restore your sense of control after a traumatic event.

What you can do. If you've experienced a traumatic event, assume that things might be rough for you for a while. Be gentle with yourself, and take time to heal. If you've experienced a loss, allow yourself time to mourn, and don't be too hard on yourself during this period. It's not unusual to feel shame, guilt, or even numbness after a traumatic event. Many people feel angry at themselves and wonder if they could have done more to avoid the trauma. Don't be afraid to ask for help from people who love you and who will listen and empathize. If you can be relaxed about this, talk about your experience with family or close friends. If that feels too uncomfortable, try keeping a diary of your thoughts and feelings or check out local support groups designed to help people who have experienced a trauma. Sometimes it's easier to talk to people you don't know well. If you want to visit a group, look for one led by a trained and experienced professional.

As you're getting better, live as healthy a life as possible so your body can better cope with the inevitable stress. It may be tempting to try deadening your anger, emotional pain, or stress with alcohol and drugs, but this will only worsen your problems. Get lots of rest and exercise and eat healthy, well-balanced meals at regular times. Keeping to a routine can be especially important if your normal everyday routines have been disrupted, especially if you experienced a natural disaster or are forced to live temporarily away from home. Take some time off and try to keep up with a hobby or something fun.

You may not feel like you have a lot to give right now, but see if you can volunteer and help someone else. Reaching out to others in difficult situations can help provide a sense of control and help you feel positive about yourself.

Depending on the traumatic event, most teens will gradually recover without treatment within six months, but don't be surprised if serious problems persist for longer and interfere with your daily life. Overwhelming nervousness or lingering melancholy can affect your schoolwork, your family life, and your friendships. Unfortunately, many people with PTSD don't get help because they don't realize that their uncomfortable symptoms are connected to their traumatic experience. Moreover, many traumatized people just don't feel like talking about their problems, because dealing with anything related to the event makes them feel even more uncomfortable.

If this is happening to you, it's best to talk with your parents about visiting an experienced mental health professional who can help you deal with your response to extreme stress.

At the therapist's office. Mental health professionals are trained to work with teens who have been affected by trauma and help them find constructive ways of dealing with the emotional impact. Therapists use a combination of medications and careful psychotherapy to help people suffering from PTSD.

Psychotherapy. Cognitive-behavioral therapy is the most effective approach in treating PTSD. It involves working with both the teen's thoughts and behavior. Typically, therapy begins with the teen discussing the traumatic event. Next, the therapist might teach some relaxation and assertiveness training techniques that can help the teen manage anxiety while learning how to correct distorted thoughts related to the trauma.

That's how I worked with Lee, a 20-year old-college student who had been terrorized by his father as a child and beaten by teachers in his native China. As a result of these early experiences, Lee feared others—especially those in positions of power. He also suffered from low self-worth, believing himself incapable of doing anything right. He was hypersensitive to any type of criticism and would quickly get angry if corrected. In treatment, we used cognitive therapy to improve his opinions about himself.

Although not everyone agrees about the advisability of exposing children and teens to the events that traumatized them, exposure-based treatments seem to help in situations where memories or reminders are distressing. During exposure therapy, the teen is exposed gradually to the disturbing event and taught to relax while recalling the details. Through this procedure, the teen learns not to fear his or her memories. This type of therapy also can also help convince a child that she or he really is safe in the world.

It worked well with Lee, who was gradually desensitized to situations where he anticipated rejection. As we worked together, he began to anticipate situations of possible rejection and learned to handle this type of criticism. Over the weeks of treatment, he successfully learned how to cope with this type of criticism and became far more confident in these situations. He was able to continue in school and became a doctoral candidate in physics at a large university.

Treatment is often paired with family therapy, so that your therapist can help your parents understand your PTSD symptoms. In fact, research shows that the better your parents can support you, the quicker you'll recover. In addition, many therapists use a process of guided discovery to help the person evaluate the belief that he or she has been irreversibly damaged as a result of the event.

It's not unusual for kids to criticize themselves for not handling a situation better or at least differently. Many kids feel terribly guilty about this. During treatment, they need help to be freed from the guilt, to be reassured that they did everything they could have done under the circumstances, and to understand that they had no control over being the victim, that it could have happened to anyone.

That's what worked with Kate, a teenage girl who had been raped several times by different people on different occasions. As a result, she was plagued with violent nightmares and daily, obsessive thoughts about the rapes. Eventually she grew to hate men and became quite aggressive toward them. She also began using drugs and cutting herself to escape constant thoughts about her traumas. Although her family supported her after the rapes, she didn't believe they truly cared about her, and she felt as if she was dealing with the trauma all alone. Deep inside, she believed that she couldn't protect herself and that the world was an unsafe place. As a result, she thought about killing herself and constantly put herself in dangerous situations. She believed that because of the rapes, she was permanently damaged. Her personality, her energy, and her interest in life vanished, and she felt alone and abandoned.

Therapy was a valuable outlet for her. One of the things she needed was the opportunity to tell her story and to believe that someone really understood what she'd been going through. During the first few sessions, Kate and I discussed her belief about being "damaged goods." She was physically healthy, I pointed out, and although she was psychologically wounded, the rapes were not something that had to change the course of her life in the sense of what kind of career she might have, where she would live, or who her friends would be. There were still a lot of things she could control. In addition, Kate learned relaxation techniques and was encouraged to get out and get lots of physical exercise, which she used to enjoy. All of this occurred within a relatively short time. Within a month and a half, she was able to stop thinking about the rapes all the time, and her nightmares had significantly decreased.

She learned that she would probably have an occasional nightmare but that she didn't have to let it throw her life off track. It was a painful memory but not something that would render her helpless. As she began to feel better, she discontinued her high-risk behaviors and stopped using drugs.

Medication.   In some cases, a brief course of medication in addition to therapy can be helpful. Studies have found that several types of medication, particularly the selective serotonin reuptake inhibitors and other antidepressants, can be effective in PTSD. These medications help ease serious symptoms of depression and anxiety, helping you cope with school and the pressures of everyday life while you work with your therapist. Medication is often used as a temporary measure until people with PTSD feel better.

WHAT YOU NEED TO KNOW

▸ Post-traumatic stress disorder (PTSD) is a condition that occurs after someone experiences a traumatic, potentially life-threatening event, triggering frightening thoughts and memories and emotional numbness.

▸ PTSD can be caused by a violent mugging or rape, being kidnapped or held captive, child abuse, serious car accidents, or natural disasters like floods or earthquakes.

▸ The hippocampus (a part of the brain that helps encode information into memories and processes traumatic events) is often smaller in people who have been abused or who have served in a war, which could explain why individuals with post-traumatic stress disorder have flashbacks, memory problems, and fragmented memories of the traumatic event.

▸ Genes also can make a person more susceptible to PTSD.

▸ The three main symptoms associated with PTSD are flashbacks or nightmares, avoiding places or events related to the trauma, and feeling numb.

▸ Other symptoms may include fear, anxiety, depression, self-destructive behavior, feelings of isolation, poor self-esteem, difficulty trusting others, substance abuse, acting out, poor schoolwork, and dropping grades.

▸ Symptoms usually begin within three months and last for at least a month; some kids recover within six months, but others have symptoms that last much longer. In some cases, the condition may be chronic.

▸ Typically, symptoms are worse as a result of deliberate trauma (such as rape or assault).

▸ Therapists use a combination of medications and careful psychotherapy to help people suffering PTSD.

▸ Cognitive-behavioral therapy is the most effective approach in treating PTSD and involves working with both the teen's thoughts and behavior.

➤ Treatment is often paired with family therapy to help your parents understand your symptoms; the better your parents can support you, the quicker you'll recover.
➤ In some cases, a brief course of medication in addition to therapy can be helpful.

7

"I Worry All the Time!":
Generalized Anxiety Disorder (GAD)

Ed was a 13-year-old boy who worried about every-thing. A top student, he was never satisfied with his grades. With each A he earned, the pressure to continue doing well only increased. But his worries didn't stop there; he also worried that he didn't have a girlfriend and that he wasn't good at sports. He kept wondering if he was getting cancer and whether his mother would start dating now that she was divorced from his father. He even worried about how much he worried. Many days, he stayed home from school because of stomach pains or headaches, but even when he huddled in bed the worries never went away.

Eventually, his concerns spiraled so out of control that his mother took him for an evaluation. The diagnosis was generalized anxiety disorder (GAD).

Everybody worries about silly things now and again, but there's a difference between occasional butterflies in the stomach over an upcoming test or whether you'll have a date for the prom and excessive, uncontrollable, and unrealistic worries that interfere with your daily life. Teens with GAD worry about everything, all the time—grades, homework, sports, boyfriends, or girlfriends. They are also likely to experience physical symptoms, such as trembling, muscular aches, insomnia, abdominal upset, dizziness, or irritability.

However, because the symptoms of GAD aren't quite as dramatic as some of the other anxiety disorders—for example, you probably won't experience panic attacks—it can be harder to diagnose. Traditionally, a doctor can confirm the condition if you've been struggling with constant worries about many things for most days in the past six months.

Everybody worries, but generalized anxiety disorder is much more than normal anxiety. If you have GAD, you're anxious all the time— your whole day is filled with exaggerated worry and unnecessary tension. You're always anticipating a disaster. Maybe you're worrying about your health, whether your family has enough money, whether your parents are going to get a divorce, or how well you're doing in school. The source of the worry for some teens is hard to track down. Just the thought of getting up and making it through the day triggers anxiety.

Generalized anxiety disorder usually affects children between the ages of six and 11 and generally affects more girls than guys.

HOW DO YOU KNOW YOU HAVE IT?

Symptoms of generalized anxiety disorder don't normally occur all at once. You may begin feeling a bit anxious at some point between late childhood and early adolescence. Then the worries just keep building and building, until you're constantly worrying about everything— drowning in what-ifs—day after day. Children with GAD tend to be very hard on themselves as they try to be perfect, sometimes redoing tasks over and over, while they also look to others for constant approval or reassurance.

That's the situation with Brad, who at age 12 was still sleeping in his parents' bedroom because he feared being separated from them and worried that they might hurt themselves or get sick. After all, he reasoned, you never knew if something would happen or go wrong. Brad and other kids like him just assume that bad things will happen.

Most teens with GAD worry about the big things—school success, finances, family issues—but they'll also worry about little things, like whether they'll get their chores done and finish their homework or whether they're going to be late for school tomorrow. It may feel like you just can't stop worrying, yet most likely you realize that your anxiety is way more intense than it should be. In fact, that's how most teens describe GAD: "I just can't seem to turn my mind off," they say. "I just keep dwelling on every little thing." They realize something is wrong but can't get control over it. If a friend is a few minutes late, the person with GAD might think, "Oh, no! There must have been an accident. What am I going to do?" or "They're not going to show up! That must mean they don't like me."

Most teens with GAD also have physical symptoms. You may feel tired all the time, or you may have headaches, concentration problems, muscle aches or tension, a tight throat, trembling, twitching, irritability, sweating, or hot flashes. You might feel lightheaded, out of breath, or nauseated. Some teens have to go to the bathroom more often than normal. If you have GAD, you probably have a hard time relaxing, and you may get startled more easily than other people. You also may have difficulty concentrating and falling or staying asleep.

However, unlike people with other types of anxiety disorders, teens with GAD don't usually avoid certain situations as a result of their disorder. In mild cases, you may still be able to function in school and in social settings, and you may be able to hold down an after-school job. In more severe cases, however, the problem makes it hard to get up in the morning or carry on even the easiest daily activities. You might have trouble imagining how you can get through the day or worry that you can't possibly have enough strength or stamina to deal with all the challenges that are going to come your way.

People with GAD are worriers, and they typically come from families of worriers. They worry about what people will think or won't think, about what will or won't happen. They just worry all the time.

That pretty much describes David, 17, a high school junior who had never been the sort of kid to be picked first for the neighborhood softball team. He wasn't very athletic, but he was brainy. Having no athletic ability and getting all A's earned him lots of teasing, jeering, and harassment from other kids. By the time he came to therapy, he was a fast thinker, prompted by a high level of anxiety. He was hypervigilant about everything and had a tendency to fly off the handle. Because he worried so much, when things didn't go the way he wanted he felt out of control and irritable. He also had a poor self-image because he had experienced so much rejection by his peers. As time went on, he'd started giving up, because he believed that no matter what he did he wasn't good enough to make it right—to fix things. He thought nobody liked him, and he thought he was unable to change that situation. He anticipated disaster in everything, believed the future held nothing good for him, and pretty much dreaded the rest of his life. On top of this, his anxiety contributed to constant physical discomfort that cost him a lot of time away from school and activities. There were so many things that could go wrong that he didn't really have control over, and he felt stuck.

His basic underlying conviction was that something bad was going to happen, because nothing ever went right for him." When I asked him if he'd ever had a good time or if he could remember when he felt peaceful, he replied that he'd never felt that way in his life. He'd always felt anxious, and he had no idea what it was like to feel

Do You Have Generalized Anxiety Disorder (GAD)?

If you think you might have GAD, fill out the checklist below to assess the extent of your symptoms. Then show the results to your mental health professional.

Do you have

☐ constant worries most days, for the past six months?

☐ unreasonable worries about your health?

☐ unreasonable worries about your school performance?

☐ uncontrollable worries?

Do you have at least three of the following frequent physical symptoms?

☐ headaches

☐ stomachaches

☐ swallowing problems

☐ tight throat

☐ trembling or twitching

☐ sleep problems

☐ sweating

☐ nausea or vomiting

☐ lightheadedness or weakness

☐ irritability

☐ muscle weakness

☐ fatigue

☐ worries that interfere with your everyday life

relaxed, calm, or peaceful. First, we had to evaluate his automatic thought: Is it true that there's no place that's safe? He insisted that every place posed a threat. Instead, I asked him to identify places that weren't absolutely safe but certainly safer than others. He admitted there were places he could go where he would be safer.

Next, we discussed whether it was true that nothing ever went right and that everything went wrong. He said no, because he lived in a family of, for the most part, supportive, successful, middle-class people. He went to school, he did well, he had a lot of support and talent, and in those regards it wasn't true that nothing ever went right or was in his favor. Eventually, he was able to recognize that things sometimes did go right.

The central part of treatment for David was relaxation. Because he couldn't think of a relaxing place, we did deep muscle relaxation and deep breathing. Because he had such a high level of activity and energy, I recommended he listen to music, read, or take walks. As he did those things, his overall level of anxiety dropped, and he became less irritable.

During therapy, he would imagine himself in situations where things didn't go well or the way he wanted. He imagined himself performing in difficult situations, and he imagined that he tolerated the situation well. Thus, he would not anticipate the worst thing that would happen but would imagine it would turn out okay.

After six months of therapy, David was less anxious, less irritable, and less sensitive to various situations and therefore better adjusted at school and at home. As his anxiety level dropped, his social skills improved, and other kids interacted with him in a friendlier way.

COEXISTING CONDITIONS

If you have GAD along with another anxiety disorder, depression, or substance abuse, these other conditions must be treated at the same time, but treatment becomes more complex with multiple disorders.

That was the case with Michael, who started worrying about everything in early childhood. By the time he reached middle school, he was having many social problems, which didn't help his constant worrying. When a couple of classmates introduced him to alcohol and other drugs, he was eager to try them. He found that alcohol eased some of his worries and calmed his nerves, so he started to drink—a lot. By the time he was a teenager, drinking was getting Michael into trouble. He skipped school almost every week, and when he wasn't skipping he was home sick with stomachaches and headaches. He found it more and more difficult to concentrate. He now had a serious alcohol problem on top of his anxiety issues. Although drinking appeared to ease his anxiety, it only replaced those nervous feelings with another set of serious problems. Even worse, he discovered that when he stopped drinking, the anxiety always remained lurking right beneath the surface, because he had never dealt with it effectively.

CAUSE

Experts believe that GAD is caused by a combination of brain chemistry, life events, personality, and genetics. This means that it's not your fault if you have GAD.

Brain. The biochemical basis of GAD begins in the brain. Several parts of your brain play important parts in a complex interaction that triggers fear and anxiety. Using brain scans and other techniques, scientists have tracked down a network of areas in the brain that appear to be responsible. One of the most important parts of this network is the amygdala, an almond-shaped structure deep within the brain that controls communication between the parts of the brain that process incoming sensory signals and the parts that interpret them. The amygdala can interpret something as a threat and trigger an anxiety or fear response. Emotional memories seem to be stored in the central part of the amygdala, which may play a role in disorders involving very distinct fears, such as phobias. Other forms of anxiety are triggered by other parts of the brain.

Heredity. If a close relative of yours has GAD, you have a 20 percent higher risk for developing the condition. You have a 10 percent risk of having GAD if your relatives are diagnosed with depression (there seems to be a link between GAD and other psychiatric disorders, including depression, phobia disorder, and panic disorder). GAD also affects about twice as many girls as guys.

Life stress. In addition to a family history, you may be at higher risk of developing GAD if you're stressed about school or home issues and you haven't been getting enough sleep. This is particularly a problem at the beginning of middle school and the onset of puberty, as you have to cope with hormonal changes, different social expectations, and early dating. These things give kids something new to worry about. While some will be able to handle the extra stress, others feel overwhelmed and completely unprepared.

DIAGNOSIS

It's normal for kids and teens to get nervous or anxious about things going on in their life or in the world; such worries don't mean you have GAD. You shouldn't be concerned about being a little anxious now and then; after all, most people face some anxiety in their daily lives.

However, GAD is more likely to occur during middle childhood and adolescence. If your anxiety is overwhelming, persistent, or begins to interfere with everyday life, you may want to ask your parents to schedule an appointment for you with a psychotherapist for a professional diagnosis. If you've spent at least six months worrying excessively about a number of everyday problems, you've probably got GAD.

HOW IS IT TREATED?

Fortunately, up to 90 percent of people with GAD can be effectively treated, so that they can go on to live a full and productive life. In fact, GAD can be completely overcome in about three to four months if you're motivated and work hard to recover. It's important to treat GAD, because research has shown that kids with untreated GAD are more likely to perform poorly in school, have weaker social skills, and be more vulnerable to substance abuse.

Psychotherapy. The best treatment for GAD is cognitive-behavioral therapy—a type of active psychotherapy in which you slowly change the way you look at situations and problems. At the same time, during CBT you'll also learn methods and techniques to reduce anxiety. Because it's hard for some teens with GAD to calm down enough to experience quiet, peaceful moments, strategies to calm down and relax are another part of overcoming this problem.

Medication. Sometimes medication is added as a part of this treatment, but for many teens it isn't necessary. In particular, the selective serotonin reuptake inhibitors (SSRIs) escitalopram (Lexapro), venlafaxine (Effexor), and paroxetine (Paxil) have been approved for treatment of GAD. There are current studies indicating that the tricyclic antidepressant imipramine and other SSRIs also may be effective for general anxiety. The SSRIs citalopram (Celexa), fluvoxamine (Luvox), fluoxetine (Prozac), and sertraline (Zoloft) are often useful. Other new antidepressants, such as duloxetine (Cymbalta), venlafaxine (Effexor), or mirtazapine (Remeron), also might help.

Other drugs commonly prescribed are buspirone (BuSpar) and several of the benzodiazepines, such as diazepam (Valium), alprazolam (Xanax), lorazepam (Ativan), oxazepam (Serax), and chlordiazepoxide (Librium). If the anxious patient is able to wait for the benefits of the medication for two to four weeks, buspirone is often a good first choice. However, if a quicker response is needed, the benzodiazepines may be more appropriate. However, there is a particular concern about the use of benzodiazepines because of their potential for physical dependence. Antihistamines also are sometimes used to treat GAD.

IN THE FUTURE

By learning more about brain circuitry involved in fear and anxiety, scientists may be able to devise new and more specific treatments for anxiety disorders. For example, someday scientists may be able to increase the influence of the thinking parts of the brain on the amygdala, so that a person can consciously control fear and anxiety. Although studies of twins suggest that genes play a role in anxiety disorders, heredity alone can't explain what causes these problems in the first place. Your experiences also play a part. Researchers are trying to learn how genetics and experience interact in people with GAD so they can learn how to better treat or even prevent the problem.

WHAT YOU NEED TO KNOW

➤ Teens with generalized anxiety disorder (GAD) worry about everything, all the time, and are likely to experience physical symptoms such as trembling, muscular aches, insomnia, abdominal upset, dizziness, or irritability.

➤ GAD is much more than normal anxiety; it can be diagnosed if you've been struggling with constant worries about lots of different things for most days in the past six months.

➤ GAD usually affects children between the ages of six and 11 and generally affects more girls than guys.

➤ Symptoms begin slowly, with mild feelings of anxiety between late childhood and early adolescence; worries keep building until you're constantly worrying.

➤ Experts believe that GAD is caused by a combination of brain chemistry, life events, personality, and genetics.

➤ Up to 90 percent of people with GAD can be effectively treated in three to four months if they're motivated and work hard to recover.

➤ The best treatment for GAD is cognitive-behavioral therapy, a type of active psychotherapy in which you slowly change the way you look at situations and problems. You'll also learn methods and techniques to reduce anxiety and to relax.

➤ Sometimes medication is added as a part of this treatment, but for many teens it isn't necessary.

"I Think I'm Going to Die!":
Anxiety to the Extreme—
Panic Disorder

Brittany was a 15-year-old soccer star who experienced her first panic attack while shopping at the mall. She was picking out shoes with some friends when she suddenly thought she was having a heart attack. Her heart started to pound, and her hands shook so much she could hardly put her wallet back in her purse. Sweat broke out on her upper lip, and she felt as if her throat was closing up.

After that first attack, she became much more reluctant to go back to the mall, fearing a recurrent attack might embarrass her in front of her friends. She also became afraid of driving over bridges and riding in elevators out of fear of triggering an attack.

Brittany was struggling with panic disorder and has since suffered severe attacks of panic that make her feel as if she's having a heart attack or is going crazy. Her symptoms include heart palpitations, chest pain or discomfort, sweating, trembling, tingling sensations, feeling of choking, fear of dying or losing control, and feelings of unreality.

Once you start to panic, it's easy to get trapped in a vicious cycle of symptoms and panic, panic and more symptoms. Affecting twice as many girls as guys, panic disorder typically starts during late adolescence, and the risk of developing the condition may be inherited.

Many people with panic disorder experience *situational avoidance*—which means that you avoid the place you were visiting or event you were participating in when the panic attack occurred. If you were shopping, you avoid malls. If you were driving, you stop riding in cars. Some teen's lives become so restricted that they avoid all normal, everyday activities, or they might be able to confront a feared situation only if accompanied by a parent or other trusted person.

In extreme cases, people worry so much about experiencing a panic attack that they avoid any situation in which they would feel helpless if a panic attack were to occur. In about one-third of panic attack cases, a person's life becomes so restricted that he or she doesn't want to leave the house for fear of having an attack. This condition is called *agoraphobia* and develops as a result of the fear of another panic attack, not from fear of an object or event. Early treatment of panic disorder can often prevent agoraphobia from developing.

Elizabeth had a frightening experience as a young child during a special program at a local sports club for kids when an unknown adult grabbed her hand when the group was asked to join hands and form a circle. The next day, she refused to enter the clubroom. The day after that, she became frightened when she saw the other kids in the class milling around outside the clubroom. The next time she was scheduled to go to the club, she refused to attend. Eventually, even the sight of another child—any child—set off a panic attack. Each day, her fears gradually became more general, but they were all traced back to the original unpleasant experience.

An initial panic attack experienced under specific circumstances can quickly generate more general fears. If a panic attack strikes while you're shopping in the mall, you may develop a fear of crowds, the store you were in, or the entire mall. If you experience a panic attack while riding in an elevator, you may develop a fear of elevators. If you start avoiding crowds, or the mall, or elevators, it affects your choice of a job or apartment and greatly restricts other parts of your life. Imagine turning down a dream job on the 43rd floor of a New York City office building because of your fear of riding in an elevator.

Following a panic attack, some people fear having another one in a place from which escape would be difficult. Often they keep avoiding such places and any place they fear might spark a panic attack until there are very few places left where they feel comfortable outside their own home.

That's what happened to Sam, one of my clients, who was a 15-year-old high school sophomore when his panic disorder developed into agoraphobia. Sam had always tended to stay close to home, but the situation had worsened to the point that he wouldn't go out alone. Brief jaunts, such as going to the mall, were out of the question. Sam left the house only when he absolutely had to. He realized he had to go to school, but he took many sick days. Because he didn't have many friends, he was very dependent on his parents, who drove him to places he had to go, did his errands, and generally took care of him. It's very hard for someone with agoraphobia to live alone.

Sam had particular problems when he was in the spotlight, such as if someone in a store asked him a question, even something as harmless as "May I help you?" In these situations he started to feel as if he was choking. His head spun, he felt trapped, and he believed he was going to pass out. His worst fear was that when he started to panic, his symptoms would continue to get worse until he lost consciousness. He always declined when his mom asked him to go with her to the store, because he worried that the car would break down and leave them stranded and that he'd be trapped and unable to do anything about it. Sam was, in fact, trapped by his panic disorder.

WHAT CAUSES IT?

Several factors can play a role in the development of anxiety conditions such as panic disorder. There seems to be a connection between the development of a panic disorder and a significant loss or a major, stressful transition such as moving, going to a new school, or graduating. In addition, the disorder may be influenced by genetics; studies with twins have confirmed that panic disorder may be inherited. Brain malfunctions also may be a factor, although a specific brain problem has not yet been identified.

The symptoms of panic are caused by the overactivity of the body's normal fear response. The symptoms that you feel during a panic attack are typical of your body's normal fight-or-flight response, something that anyone would experience in a life-or-death situation. If a mountain lion suddenly appeared out of the bushes in your backyard, it's likely that your heart would start to pound, your stomach would knot, and you'd start breathing more quickly as your body prepared itself to fight or to run away from danger. If you were facing a predator, those symptoms would make perfect sense.

Your body's fight-or-flight response becomes a problem when it kicks in when there isn't a life-or-death situation. During a panic attack, these symptoms appear out of the blue, in apparently harmless situations such as shopping, taking a walk, or even sleeping.

Life experiences and learned behavior also play a part in the development of a panic disorder. Although initial panic attacks may come out of the blue, eventually you help trigger them yourself by responding to physical symptoms of an attack. Let's say you have panic disorder and your heart starts to pound after you've run a few laps around the ball field in gym. If you interpret your racing heartbeat as a symptom of an attack, the anxiety you feel can trigger a real panic attack. Of course, sometimes exercise (along with certain medications, coffee, and so on) can cause a panic attack itself. It can be hard to tell the difference, which is why thorough treatment by a mental health professional is so important.

WHAT IT FEELS LIKE

In the throes of a panic attack, teens often report that they feel as if they are losing control, that they can't get their breath or get enough air, and that they have an overwhelming feeling that things are caving in on them. During a panic attack, your heart pounds and you may feel sweaty, weak, faint, or dizzy. Your hands may tingle or feel numb, and you might feel hot, flushed, or cold. You may feel sick to your stomach. Some kids feel as if they're smothering, while others feel a sense of impending doom or loss of control. You may be convinced that you're having a heart attack, going crazy, or going to pass out or die. The terror can be paralyzing. And when teens with panic disorder aren't having an attack, they're worrying about when the next one will occur.

You can experience a panic attack anywhere, any time—even while you're sound asleep. And while it may seem to last a lifetime, most panic attacks typically peak within 10 minutes. Your body simply can't sustain the fight-or-flight response for longer than that.

If you have panic disorder, you know that the terrified feeling can strike with no warning, out of the blue. Because you can't predict when an attack will occur, you might feel very anxious between episodes, just waiting for the next one to come. Eventually, the world begins to shrink, and you may ultimately develop agoraphobia.

Of course, not everyone who experiences panic attacks will develop a full-blown panic disorder. For example, many teens have just one panic attack and never suffer another. If you've had just one or two,

Coexisting Conditions

Just like many other anxiety disorders, panic disorder often occurs along with other serious conditions, such as phobias, depression, drug abuse, and alcoholism, and sometimes can lead to suicide.

you're probably fine. The key symptom of panic disorder is the persistent fear of having more panic attacks in the future. If you've had four or more panic attacks (and especially if you are scared about having more panic attacks after the first few), you should consider finding a mental health professional who specializes in panic or anxiety disorders.

DIAGNOSIS

If you think you might have panic disorder, you need to find a licensed psychologist or other mental health professional who specializes in the diagnosis and treatment of panic and anxiety disorders. There may be a clinic nearby that specializes in these conditions. On your first appointment, you should tell the therapist that you think you have panic disorder and ask about the person's experience treating this disorder. You have a right to ask these questions.

Even if you think you have panic disorder, however, you can't diagnose yourself. An experienced mental health specialist is the best person to make this diagnosis and treat this problem.

TREATMENT

If you've been diagnosed with panic disorder, you'll be glad to hear that it's one of the most treatable of all of the anxiety disorders. The condition responds in most cases to a combination of medication and carefully targeted psychotherapy. It's important to get treatment, however, because if you don't, the disorder can eventually get in the way of your life. Many teens with panic disorder visit the hospital emergency room more and more often (fearing they're suffering a heart attack), or they see a number of doctors before they are correctly diagnosed. Some people with panic disorder may go for years without learning that they have a real, treatable illness.

The first step in treatment is simply to learn as much as you can about panic disorder, and the health expert you visit will help explain the problem to you. Simply learning that you're not crazy and you're not going to have a heart attack can be very reassuring.

Cognitive-behavioral therapy. Cognitive-behavioral therapy can be very effective in treating people with panic disorder. It focuses on helping you change your thinking in a process called *cognitive restructuring*. With this method, you'll learn how to replace the panicky automatic thought you have ("I'm going to die!") with more realistic thoughts ("This will only last a few minutes.").

To eliminate damaging automatic thoughts, you've got to figure out what core beliefs lie behind these thoughts and then change those beliefs. This is a challenging task, because changing the way you think can mean undoing years of distorted automatic thought patterns. And truly reprogramming what you think about yourself at the core of your being ("I'm incompetent") isn't as easy as it might seem.

For example, your therapist might help you identify possible triggers for the attacks—perhaps a thought or a physical sensation (shakiness, sweat, weakness). Once you understand that the panic attack is separate from the trigger, the trigger begins to lose some of its power to trigger an attack.

The behavioral part of CBT focuses on changing your reactions to anxiety-provoking situations and handling the stress that arises during these situations. In the case of panic disorder, your therapist might help you focus on exposing yourself to the physical sensations you feel during a panic attack. People with panic disorder are more afraid of the actual attack than they are of specific objects or events. While someone with a phobia about planes is truly afraid the plane will crash, people with panic disorder triggered by air travel are not afraid that the plane will crash but that they'll have a panic attack in a plane where they can't get help. As a result, they feel trapped and claustrophobic.

If you have panic disorder, exposure therapy can help you get through the symptoms of a panic attack in a controlled setting. One very effective type of exposure treatment is to break down a fearful situation (that is, a situation where you had a panic attack in the past) into baby steps and perform them one at a time. The therapist will help you teach your body to remain relaxed in situations that used to induce feelings of anxiety and will show you how to cope with panic using techniques such as relaxation or breathing skills. Using these skills, you can prevent your anxiety symptoms from developing into a full-blown panic attack as you practice these baby steps. Some experts have found that people with panic disorder tend to have slightly faster than average breathing rates, so learning to slow down your breathing also can help you deal with a panic attack and prevent future attacks.

Sam, the teenager with agoraphobia discussed earlier in this chapter, learned how to overcome his panic disorder and agoraphobia during a carefully structured series of therapy sessions. First, I taught him how to relax, and then I asked him to imagine a beautiful, safe place. When it was time for Sam to go outside, he would practice his relaxation exercises before he left the house. Once he went out, he could continue to visit his imaginary safe place in his mind to stay calm during the trip. Often he was able to prevent physical symptoms from starting by using these techniques. If he did start to feel anxious, he'd mentally imagine his safe place to deal with symptoms.

Also during our sessions, I helped Sam evaluate his belief that he'd pass out from panic: "What's the worst thing that could happen if you go outside?" As we discussed his certainty that he'd get so panicky he would pass out, I pointed out that it's impossible to pass out from a panic attack because when you panic you're hyperstimulated—your heart races and you breathe quickly. In order to pass out, your body must be understimulated—your heart rate slows down, your breathing slows down. That's the opposite of what happens when you panic.

Then I asked him, "What's the best that might happen?" He decided that the best that could happen when he went outside is that he would use his new relaxation tools and wouldn't panic. He'd have to work at not getting anxious, but he could do it by using imagery to prevent symptoms when they occurred.

He went home to practice working on his relaxation and imagery. First, he went outside on short drives and practiced his techniques. Then he started to go to a store or business. Once he was able to master this without panic, he drove in heavy traffic and then where there were long traffic lines. Finally, he practiced his techniques by attending a meeting or keeping an appointment. Sam made continuous improvement and was able to travel further from home each day. He spent more time going out, found he was able to enjoy being away from home, and found that he could do more fun things. He skipped school much less often.

During your treatment, your therapist will probably assign "homework"—specific problems that you'll need to work on between sessions. Exposure will be carried out only when you're ready and will be done gradually and only with your permission. You'll work with the therapist to determine how much you can handle and at what pace you can proceed.

One technique used by skilled clinicians is to induce a panic attack intentionally in a controlled situation. Using this procedure, the therapist leads the person into a panic attack in his or her office. The person experiences all the physical discomfort and distorted thoughts that typically happen during a panic attack while the therapist is standing by. As a result, the person learns several important things. First, the person realizes that it's possible to tolerate the physical discomfort. Next, the person realizes that no real harm occurs during a panic attack. Finally, by going through the process, the person gets positive proof that he or she won't die or go insane during a panic attack.

Inducing a panic attack worked well for Sam, who was able to understand that when he experienced a full-blown panic attack, he wouldn't pass out. This reinforced the idea that even if he has a panic attack, he will be fine.

Medication. Your doctor may prescribe medications to boost your motivation to face your panic and all of the scary baggage that goes along with it. Drugs for panic disorder may help with one of two stages of panic: when you're anticipating anxiety or during the panic attack itself. Some medicines may help ease symptoms during one or both of these stages. But the odds are that if a drug can block the panic itself, you probably won't continue to fear certain events with so much anxiety. You'll find that you can face a situation and not experience panic and that the situation isn't really dangerous at all.

The most common medications doctors use for panic disorder are antidepressants, such as Prozac, called selective serotonin reuptake inhibitors (SSRIs) and the benzodiazepines (sometimes these two groups are used together). Studies suggest that antidepressants used to help treat panic can help 75 to 80 percent of people feel better.

The tricyclic antidepressant imipramine (Tofranil) has been used for the longest time for panic disorder; other tricyclics that can help control panic attacks include

➤ amitriptyline (Elavil)
➤ clomipramine (Anafranil)
➤ desipramine (Norpramin or Pertofrane)
➤ doxepin (Sinequan or Adapin)
➤ nortriptyline (Aventyl or Pamelor)

Some of the new SSRIs have been shown to be just as effective as the tricyclics, but with fewer side effects. These include

➤ citalopram (Celexa)
➤ escitalopram (Lexapro)
➤ fluoxetine (Prozac)
➤ fluvoxamine (Luvox)
➤ paroxetine (Paxil)
➤ sertraline (Zoloft)

Monoamine oxidase inhibitors (MAOIs) are another group of antidepressants that can treat panic; doctors prefer phenelzine (Nardil), but tranylcypromine (Parnate) also is sometimes used, and there is a new transdermal MAOI, selegiline (Emsam).

The most common benzodiazepines for panic attacks are alprazolam (Xanax) and clonazepam (Klonopin), both of which block panic attacks more quickly than the antidepressants do. Users often see results within a week. These two drugs also tend to have fewer side effects than the antidepressants, but both can trigger withdrawal symptoms. Because Xanax acts more quickly than Klonopin, it's a good choice to take right before an event that you think will provoke panic. It takes about 15 to 20 minutes to work and will work much more quickly if you can stand letting it dissolve under your tongue, but it has a bitter taste. Because Klonopin lasts longer in the body than Xanax, you can take it twice a day for full 24-hour coverage, whereas you would need to take four or five doses of Xanax during the same period. A few studies suggest that diazepam (Valium) and lorazepam (Ativan) are also effective in treating panic disorder.

Your doctor may recommend that you take a combination of a benzodiazepine and an antidepressant. Other doctors may want you to take the antidepressant daily and use a benzodiazepine when you feel at risk for an oncoming panic attack; others may suggest you take both medications together during the first month of treatment, slowly tapering off the benzodiazepine.

OUTLOOK

The ultimate success of treatment depends on you. Are you willing to follow your therapist's treatment plan carefully? It may involve many steps, and it's not a magic instant cure, but if you hang in there, you should start to notice an improvement in your symptoms within three or four months of weekly sessions. If you keep up with your program, you should notice a major improvement after a year.

WHAT YOU NEED TO KNOW

- ▸ Panic disorder is an anxiety disorder causing severe panic attacks, heart palpitations, chest pain or discomfort, sweating, trembling, tingling sensations, feeling of choking, fear of dying or losing control, and feelings of unreality.
- ▸ Affecting twice as many girls as guys, panic disorder typically starts during late adolescence, and the risk of developing the condition may be inherited.

➤ Many people with panic disorder avoid the places they were visiting or events they were participating in when the panic attack occurred.

➤ About one-third of panic attack cases lead to agoraphobia, in which the person's life becomes so restricted that he or she doesn't want to leave the house for fear of having an attack.

➤ Panic disorder is linked to a significant loss or a major, stressful transition such as moving, going to a new school, or graduating. It's also influenced by genetics and brain malfunctions.

➤ The symptoms of panic are caused by the overactivity of the body's normal fear response.

➤ Panic disorder often occurs along with other serious conditions, such as phobias, depression, drug abuse, alcoholism, and sometimes suicide.

➤ The condition responds in most cases to a combination of medication and carefully targeted psychotherapy.

➤ Cognitive-behavioral therapy can be very effective in treating people with panic disorder by helping replace the panicky automatic thoughts with more realistic thoughts.

➤ Medications can boost your motivation to face your panic; drugs for panic disorder may help either when you're anticipating anxiety or during the panic attack itself.

➤ The most common medications doctors use for panic disorder are antidepressants and benzodiazepines (sometimes both).

➤ Panic disorder responds to therapy within three or four months of weekly sessions.

9

Black Cats and Broken Mirrors: Specific Phobias

Let's face it—the world can be a scary place. On an international scale there's poverty, starvation, and war. At home we face terrorism, kidnappings, tornadoes, hurricanes, lightning strikes. Pit bulls might attack, and cars get in accidents. It's no surprise, then, that every child gets scared at some time. In fact, as kids go out into the world, exploring and confronting new challenges, fears are almost unavoidable.

In fact, one study found that almost half of all children between ages six and 12 had many fears. At the top of the list were fear of the dark and fear of large barking dogs. Some children are afraid of heights, thunder, or fires; others worry about burglars, kidnappers, or nuclear war. Fear of flying has been on the increase in recent years.

Linda, 10, was afraid of dogs. She didn't know exactly when it started, although she dimly recalls being bitten by a dog as a little kid. But if she so much as sees a dog walking harmlessly down the street, she freezes and breaks into a cold sweat. Coming across an unleashed dog running wild can make her cry and become immobilized with fear.

A phobia is really a fancy name for an intense, specific fear, but fear in general is normal. Lots of kids are scared of things like important tests, violent movies, or tornadoes. In fact, it makes sense to be scared of some things, such as ice storms when you're driving or a strong undertow when you're swimming in the ocean.

But some fears go way beyond normal. Some kids with specific phobias suffer from an intense fear reaction to a specific object or

121

situation (such as planes, spiders, dogs, or heights). The level of fear is usually far beyond what would be appropriate (for example, the likelihood that a plane will crash is remote). Also, this fear can lead to the avoidance of common, everyday situations. The most common specific phobia in kids and teens is the fear of animals—particularly dogs, snakes, insects, and mice. Other common phobias include storms, blood, heights, water, injections, and the dark.

Many times phobias develop in kids who are in general fairly anxious, and their phobias seem to worsen with age. Experts think about two percent of preteens have at least one phobia, and about five percent of teenagers have the problem.

Mild discomfort about a situation or specific item or animal isn't a full-blown phobia. Kids who have phobias try to avoid the objects and situations they fear, and eventually this can interfere with their lives. If your phobia interferes with your ability to go to school, hang out with your friends, or live a normal life, you should have your parents make an appointment with a mental health professional for an evaluation.

That's what Andy's parents did when they realized that his deep-seated fear of flying was going to interfere with the family's plans to vacation in Florida. Andy, age 13, had never flown before, but in the wake of the 9/11 terrorist attacks in New York City and Washington, D.C., he had developed a full-blown phobia about flying and airplanes. He decided that flying was just not safe because of the risk of terrorists, poor security at airports, and poor safety controls by the airlines. Even thinking about getting on a plane with his family sent him into hysterical fits of crying, and he absolutely refused to get on an airplane. He'd never been the kind of kid to misbehave or have temper tantrums before, so his parents suspected his bad behavior was based on his unreasonable fears. Other family members had flown safely many times, but nothing they could say to him would help; it seemed that the more they talked about flying, the worse his fears became. His automatic thought in terms of flying was that flying isn't safe, and nothing his family could say would sway him.

WHAT IT FEELS LIKE

When you have a phobia about something, encountering it can trigger feelings of panic, dread, horror, or terror that seem uncontrollable. You're unable to think of anything else as your body revs up its fight-or-flight response. Your heart pounds, you sweat and have "butterflies" in your stomach, and you may feel weak, faint, or dizzy. You might tremble or have an overwhelming desire to flee. Your hands may tingle or feel numb, and you might feel hot, flushed, or cold. You may feel sick to your stomach. Some kids feel as if they can't breathe or are suffocating, while others feel a sense of impending doom or loss of control. You may be convinced you're having a heart attack, going crazy, or dying. The terror can be paralyzing, even though in your more rational moments you know that there isn't much real danger to you.

A child or teenager who has a particularly frightening or threatening experience with an animal or a situation may develop a specific phobia. For instance, if you've been bitten by a vicious dog or witnessed someone else get bitten, you may develop a fear of all dogs, no matter how friendly. Witnessing or suffering a violent attack is another risk factor for specific phobia. Even repeatedly warning a child or teenager about a potentially dangerous situation or animal can cause a phobia. If your mother reminds you every day not to get into a stranger's car (no matter how valid the warning) eventually you may become phobic about strangers or cars.

It's also possible to learn fear from others. For instance, if your mother is very scared of spiders and screams and runs whenever she sees a spider web, even if there is no spider nearby, you could learn to respond the same way.

DIAGNOSIS

A mental health specialist can diagnose a specific phobia if the fear lasts for at least six months and interferes with your daily routine. If a fear is reasonable it cannot be classed as a phobia. Luckily, however, phobias are very common, and they aren't a sign of serious mental illness that's going to require months or years of therapy.

Before your first visit to a therapist, you'll probably be asked to have a complete physical exam to see if other health conditions could be causing your symptoms. Because phobias may appear with other anxiety disorders or with depression, substance abuse, or eating disorders, your therapist will want to rule out these problems before suggesting treatment. Then, on your first visit, your therapist will probably ask you to describe your symptoms and explain how often they occur and what triggers them. You'll be asked about any automatic thoughts that occur in relation to your phobia.

CAUSE

The causes of specific phobias aren't well understood. No one really knows why one kid who gets bitten by a dog becomes phobic and another one never thinks twice about dogs after a similar experience. Phobias are a type of anxiety disorder, and anxiety disorders can be inherited. There's some evidence that these phobias may run in families; if you have a phobia, your mother or father may have one too. You may inherit a type of personality that makes you more prone to develop a phobia: You may naturally be more careful and cautious, for example.

Sometimes a phobia develops after something awful happens in your life, such as your parents getting a divorce or a family member dying.

Some phobias can be learned. Normally, kids watch their parents to see how they react to situations and objects; this is a way of learning what's safe and what's not safe in the world. But if your parent overreacts to an object or situation, you may learn to react in the same way and develop a phobia.

Specific phobias usually first appear during childhood or adolescence and tend to last into adulthood.

TREATMENT

If the object of your fear is easy to avoid (let's say you're afraid of snakes and you live in New York City), you may not feel the need to seek treatment. But if you find yourself making important personal decisions to avoid a phobic situation, or if this avoidance is carried to extreme lengths, it can be disabling. Patterns of anxiety, avoidance, and worry about possibly experiencing the phobic situation tend to grow more severe with time and can interfere with your life. When you get older, an untreated phobia may influence your career choices. For example, you may refuse a high-paying job because it would require air travel. In these cases, it may make sense to treat and overcome your phobia.

Phobias usually respond well to psychotherapy treatment, and almost all phobia patients can completely overcome their fears. In fact, you'll be happy to hear that most kids who are treated completely overcome their fears for the rest of their lives.

Desensitization therapy. Exposure or desensitization therapy is usually the first method your therapist will select in helping you conquer your phobia. In this type of treatment, you'll work with a therapist to face the object or situation in a slow, careful, gradual way, so that you can learn how to control your physical fear symptoms. This is a type of behavior therapy, and it's a common way of overcoming phobias. It works because the brain can learn to adapt to something that seems scary but really isn't if it slowly has the chance to encounter that thing in a controlled, gradual, supported way. Gradual exposure slowly introduces someone to the feared object or situation, so that anxiety decreases as the person faces the fear—first from far away and then gradually closer and closer. Although the pace is never hurried and no one is forced to go through the steps quickly, this process can sometimes be accomplished in just a couple of sessions.

First, your therapist will teach you relaxation or breathing techniques designed to help you relax while you're imagining or encountering the object. Relaxation techniques may include things such as muscle relaxation training, deep breathing, guided mental imagery, or soothing self-talk. The reason you learn how to relax before facing your phobia is simple: It's impossible for you to feel fear and relaxation at the same time. In fact, it's impossible for you to feel fear and any other strong emotion at the same time: You can't feel fear and anger, fear and love, or fear and joy at same time. One strong emotion inhibits the other.

You've learned to fear something in the first place by being exposed to or experiencing something bad, whether that was flying, spiders, heights, or social situations. Anything you are traumatized by teaches you that exposure to this thing can be a threat. Anxiety tends to be a future-oriented feeling. We worry that something is going to happen; we worry that we're going to be confronted and won't be able to deal with it. This is different from pregame jitters or butterflies in your stomach before a performance. With a fear or phobia, you worry that a situation is going to come up and you won't have the tools you need to deal with it, so something bad might happen to you. The audience might jeer you off the stage. They might laugh. You've learned that this is a threatening situation, and as a result, you feel anxiety or fear.

The goal in therapy is first to teach you how to relax. You'd be surprised how many people don't know how to relax. Once you learn how to relax, your therapist will ask you what you're afraid of, and then the two of you will come up with 10 or 12 steps of varying intensity related to that fear. Some steps may cause only very mild feelings of discomfort, and they're the ones you'll start with. After you've mastered each of those steps individually, you'll move on to the next step and then the next, and so on until you get through all the steps. For example, if you were afraid of spiders, you'd come up with the easiest thing you could do with a spider—look at the picture of a spider in book. Then, in increasing intensity, you might get an image of a spider in your mind, look at a spider that's 50 feet away, look at a spider 10 feet away, and look at a spider two feet away. All of these steps would lead up to the final, most difficult step: holding a spider in your hand.

First, you would imagine doing each one of these things in the safety of your therapist's office. Then you actually do them, one by one. Some phobias—such as spiders—lend themselves very well to the therapist's office, but others, such as flying, do not. If you fear flying, your therapist might have a computer flight simulator in the office, or you might be sent to an airport to watch planes take off, and then perhaps take a tour of a plane, talk to an airplane mechanic, or get a tour of a control tower.

At the start of each session, you get as completely relaxed as you can be, and then you start with the least threatening item on your list. As you imagine you're in that situation, you concentrate on remaining relaxed the whole time. If you do start to feel anxious, you stop, go back, get relaxed again, and start over from the beginning. Then the therapist will give you pictures of the object or situation to look at. Once you're able to think about and look at pictures of the object or situation, your therapist will help you experience the situation or come in contact with the feared object. By confronting rather than running away from whatever scares you, you'll slowly get used to it and will overcome your terror. So, if you're really scared of snakes, first you'll be asked to think about snakes. Then you'll be shown pictures of snakes. Finally, your therapist may take you to the zoo to look at snakes behind a glass wall. Then, with a parent or a therapist at your side, you might spend a few minutes in the same room with a calm, harmless snake, such as a little garter snake. Eventually you'll be able to approach and touch a snake.

You'll keep doing that, time after time, each step of the way, until you get to the point where you are relaxing as you are being exposed to the feared object or situation itself. Eventually, you'll be able to hold a spider in your hand, give a presentation in class, or fly on an airplane, and you'll have conquered your fear.

You may do each step a minimum of three times, but this type of therapy often goes very quickly. It's not unusual to get through the entire process in just two sessions.

For example, Tammy was only nine years old, but she'd already developed a very strong fear of flying. Her fear developed a few years earlier when a plane she was flying in encountered heavy turbulence. It was a scary experience, and she felt she had no control over the plane or what was happening to her. During her treatment, we developed a list of 13 steps ranging from least disturbing (watching an airplane fly overhead while she was standing on the ground) to the most disturbing (being on a hot, crowded airplane that's being jolted around during a thunderstorm).

First, I helped Tammy feel comfortable. This part is different for everybody. Some people prefer muscle relaxation, some like to meditate, some pray, and some listen to recorded natural sounds, such as ocean waves. After Tammy learned to feel comfortable, she imagined the least disturbing step: watching the airplane fly overhead. She concentrated on being relaxed and in breathing in and out very slowly and gently. One by one, we progressed through each step until we reached the final scene: imagining being in the plane during the thunderstorm. If at any time she felt discomfort, we backed up and started again. In between sessions, Tammy practiced her relaxation exercises every day. She also learned more about the skills of airplane pilots and air traffic controllers and about how strong and safe the airplanes were. After three sessions, she was ready to fly. She went to visit family members in Texas whom she had never met before and was able to tolerate the plane flight fairly well.

Sometimes, a person is anxious or scared about something, but they are removed from their feelings and don't recognize their own anxiety. Teenagers with test anxiety may experience this as "feeling numb" or "going blank" when they begin the test. They may not feel the classic signs of anxiety, but they are suffering from anxiety all the same. If you find yourself in this situation, your therapist may ask you to imagine yourself in a test situation, paying attention to your body, noticing any tension in the muscles or any change in body temperature. You need to learn that this is the way anxiety affects you.

Cognitive-behavioral therapy is a more comprehensive form of treatment that teaches you new ways to cope with the feared object or situation. You'll learn new beliefs about the feared object or situation and the impact it has on your life. Your therapist will emphasize helping you learn how to develop a sense of mastery with your thoughts and feelings.

That's how I treated Andy, mentioned earlier in this chapter. The first thing I did during our cognitive-behavioral sessions was to address his automatic thought that flying wasn't safe, asking a series of questions designed to point out his errors in thinking: How many airplane flights are there in a day? How many people travel on airplanes every day? Which is safer, flying or driving a car? As we talked about his belief that flying wasn't safe, he began to learn that the available scientific evidence about flying didn't support his belief that flying is unsafe. In fact, most evidence about flying is that it's the safest way to travel. Scientists from the Massachusetts Institute of Technology estimate that the risk of dying in a plane crash today is one in 10 million, compared with the risk of dying in a car crash (one in 5,000) or in a train wreck (one in 400,000). According to the National Transportation and Safety Board, a passenger would have to fly 24 hours a day for more than 400 years before being involved in a fatal accident.

Next, we tackled the behavioral part of Andy's therapy. First, he learned some basic relaxation and breathing techniques. He imagined his "safe, happy place" (for Andy, it was the beach). Next, he did "homework": He traveled to his local airport to watch planes land and take off. As it turned out, his family met someone who worked at the airport, so he got a tour of a large plane and got to talk to an airplane mechanic who discussed with him all the safety features and inspections. He learned about all the plane's safety checkpoints and learned more about the control tower.

Andy left the airport with a new understanding of how many people were involved in thinking about air safety. By learning about all of these safety efforts, he realized that a lot more goes on to keep flying safe than he'd realized and that flying was probably safer than he had thought.

Next, he practiced how to prepare for the flight itself. He practiced relaxation techniques at home and assembled a few items to take along with him on the flight: a good-luck charm and a few favorite books and CDs. Shortly after our second session (it only took two), he was able to board the plane without crying and had a successful trip with his family.

Medications. It's important to understand that in cases of phobia, medications are not a successful first-choice treatment. Still, medications can be helpful in some situations. Although behavioral therapy is the main method of treatment, some research suggests that symptoms also improve with one type of antidepressant, selective serotonin reuptake inhibitors, or SSRIs, such as Prozac. These drugs help control the panic and anxiety you feel during a phobic situation. Other SSRIs used to help treat phobias include citalopram (Celexa), escitalopram (Lexapro), fluvoxamine (Luvox), paroxetine (Paxil), and sertraline (Zoloft).

A less commonly used type of antidepressant is a monoamine oxidase inhibitor (MAOI), which blocks a chemical called monoamine oxidase in the nervous system. MAOIs include phenelzine (Nardil), tranylcypromine (Parnate), selegiline (Emsam).

Benzodiazepines can help you relax and reduce your anxiety. Taking a benzodiazepine about an hour before you expect to encounter the feared object or situation can help reduce tension. If you were phobic about airplanes, you could take medication before the flight to help you manage your anxiety. The most common benzodiazepines for panic attacks are alprazolam (Xanax), clonazepam (Klonopin), lorazepam (Ativan), diazepam (Valium), and chlordiazepoxide (Librium). You'll need to use sedatives carefully because they can be addictive, but it's usually safe to use low doses of sedatives once in a while or for short periods. However, you should avoid sedatives if you have abused alcohol or drugs.

Coping skills. There are some other things you can do on your own, in addition to therapy, that can help you handle your phobia. Try not to dwell on past experiences with the situation or the object you fear; change what you can and let the rest go. If you once embarrassed yourself by screaming hysterically at school when you saw a snake, let it go. If you're feeling anxious, try to divert yourself by taking a brisk walk or immersing yourself in a hobby or a good book. Get plenty of rest and exercise, eat a balanced diet, and take time to relax. Avoid any stimulating substances that increase anxiety, such as caffeine or nicotine. Avoid alcohol and drugs. And ask your therapist about joining a support group in your area for people your age who have phobias; it can be a real boost to talk to other people with fears just like yours.

OUTLOOK

If you or someone you know has a phobia, don't turn down any chance for help. Find someone skilled in treating phobias, because the odds are in your favor: They are three to one that the treatment will succeed. Depending on your personal makeup and on how severe your phobia is, treatment can help improve your phobia within a few weeks.

WHAT YOU NEED TO KNOW

- ➤ A phobia is a fancy name for an intense, specific fear of an object or situation that is far beyond what is appropriate and that can lead to the avoidance of common, everyday situations.
- ➤ A specific phobia is diagnosed if the fear lasts for at least six months and interferes with your daily routine.
- ➤ Phobias may be learned or genetic (you may inherit a type of personality that makes you more prone to develop a phobia), or a phobia may develop after something awful happens in your life.

➤ Phobias usually respond very well to psychotherapy treatment, and almost all phobia patients can completely overcome their fears.

➤ Exposure or desensitization therapy is usually the first method to help conquer your phobia.

➤ Medications are not a successful first-choice treatment for phobias, but antidepressants or antianxiety medication may help in some situations.

10

Helping Others Cope with Anxiety

Rob has obsessive-compulsive disorder. It takes him ages to get ready for school each morning, and this often makes his younger sister Kate late for class. His rituals embarrass her, and she gets frustrated when he has to go back to the bathroom to wash his hands again before they can go to the park to play ball.

Phoebe tries to be supportive of her friend April, who's been struggling with a variety of anxiety problems for several years, but sometimes she feels exhausted. April worries about everything, and Phoebe finds herself sometimes running out of things to say to ease her friend's fears.

If one of your friends or a family member has an anxiety disorder, this probably sounds familiar. But not everyone recognizes anxiety when it happens to someone they know. When a friend or family member is struggling with an anxiety disorder, the problem may go undiagnosed for weeks, months, or even years. Not knowing what's wrong can strain your relationship, and there's no guarantee that it will improve once the problem is finally diagnosed. Remember that recovery can be a long process. There may be setbacks along the way.

IF YOU THINK THERE'S SOMETHING WRONG

Many times an anxiety disorder isn't diagnosed right away. Perhaps you've noticed that your friend doesn't seem quite the same as usual, but you're not sure what to say. If you're concerned, there's no harm in speaking up. After all, you're friends—you care about this person. You could try a caring approach, something like, *"We've been friends since sixth grade, and I think I know when something's bothering you. I've been worried about you."* Sometimes a direct question works best: *"Is everything OK? You haven't seemed like yourself lately."*

Often teenagers with anxiety disorders will turn first to their friends for help, which can put a lot of stress and responsibility on your shoulders if you've got a friend in this situation. Added to your worry about a close friend being unhappy is the burden of knowing that he or she may be seriously ill. If your friend is cutting herself in secret, should you tell? If your friend is so afraid about gaining weight that she's making herself throw up after lunch every day, do you tell? If your friend is so tired of being scared or anxious that he's considering suicide, do you notify an adult?

This is very important: If you think that your friend's actions could result in serious harm, it's your responsibility as a friend to get help for that person. It's not "ratting" or tattling—it's saving a life. Your friend may not thank you right away, but someday he or she will be grateful you stepped in.

If the person with an anxiety disorder is your mother or father, brother or sister, the problem can disrupt the entire household. Never knowing exactly what's going to happen can be very distressing. You may need to make special plans to deal with your parent's problems, or your mother, father, or sibling may not want to participate in par-

What Not to Say to Someone with an Anxiety Disorder

"Just snap out of it!"

"There's nothing to be afraid of."

"I think you're overreacting."

"Try not to worry."

"Lighten up!"

"Don't worry about it."

ties or family get-togethers. This can be frustrating and sometimes very upsetting.

Lots of people don't really understand what it means to be anxious or to have phobias, and they may react to the person's behavior with criticism. Some people mistakenly think a phobia, fear, or anxiety is just an attitude a person can change or a mood they can shake. It's not that easy. If you respond in a judgmental way, or if you immediately try to "fix" the person's anxiety, you can do more harm than good.

What you don't want to do is to make fun of the person or trivialize the disorder. It's important to understand that anxiety disorders are real. It doesn't mean the person is too lazy to get better, isn't trying hard enough, or wants to be this way. Anxiety disorders aren't a moral failing or a sign of weakness, so don't expect that the person should just be able to stop acting that way. You wouldn't be mad at your friend for having diabetes, would you? You wouldn't expect that your brother who had cancer should just get over it.

Research has uncovered evidence clearly linking many anxiety disorders, such as panic disorder and obsessive-compulsive disorder, to malfunctions of the brain's chemicals. Life's experiences and setbacks can trigger the onset of an anxiety disorder in a person who is genetically vulnerable. Anxiety disorders are illnesses too; they're conditions that a person has very little control over developing.

BEST WAYS TO HELP

If one of your friends or family members has an anxiety disorder, you can help best by being supportive and trying not to perpetuate the person's symptoms. The best way to help someone deal with anxiety issues is by listening in a caring, nonjudgmental way; make sure your friends know you're there to listen if they'd like to talk. It can be especially difficult for boys to talk about their fears.

Often, patients say one of their biggest problems is that others are reluctant or uncomfortable discussing their anxiety disorder, which makes them feel even more alone. Therefore, talk as openly and often as you can with the person and let him or her know you care. Try to be matter-of-fact and calm when you're discussing the problem. Willingness to help, patience, and trust from friends and family mean so much to the person struggling with some of these issues.

If your friend goes to a support group, you might offer to go to one of the meetings with him or her. Learn as much as you can about the disorder, so you can talk about it. Remember that people with an anxiety disorder often feel alone, so making an effort to connect can be very helpful. There's often a stigma associated with problems like this, so your friend might be reluctant to let you know what he's going through. Sometimes teens worry that you'll think their fear or behavior is silly or weird. That's why good communication is so important. You can be part of the solution, and your care and support can be valuable.

You also need to remember that there's no simple answer or magic cure. Getting better will require hard work from the person with the disorder, and a great deal of patience from you and others. But don't push a person to talk before he or she is ready—that can make things worse.

As the person struggles to overcome the anxiety disorder, there will be small gains and minor triumphs. These small victories represent major improvements, so be sure to recognize any positive step. Encourage the person to join a self-help group where he or she can share problems and achievements with others. Some people even find that participating in an Internet chat room is helpful, decreasing the person's sense of isolation. Remember, though, that any advice shared in a chat room should be viewed with caution and discussed with your therapist before you try it out.

Helping a family member. If someone in your family has an anxiety disorder, it's vital for you to learn as much as you can about the particular anxiety disorder and what you can expect. A family therapist can teach you coping mechanisms and how best to help your family member. The therapist also can intervene to lessen the

Helpful Things to Say

"It seems like you're having a hard time."

"How can I help?"

"I'll always be here for you."

"If you want to talk about it, I'll listen."

"Hang in there. I know things will get better, and I'll do anything I can to help you."

damage the person's problems cause to family relationships. It's important for you to learn when to be supportive and when to push the person to do something he or she may be reluctant to do. You may want to join family therapy if a parent or sibling has an anxiety disorder, so you can learn what to expect and how to best support the person's recovery.

Ask your parents to set up regular family meetings to help improve communication. If possible, try to talk to your family member's therapist from time to time. Be willing to be involved in family therapy if it's suggested.

Understand that there may be setbacks during stressful times. For example, if your brother has generalized anxiety disorder and your family is moving to a new school district or your parents are getting a divorce, you can expect that your brother's symptoms may temporarily worsen.

Be flexible and try to keep things as normal as possible around the house. Try to maintain a regular schedule: Get up, go to work and school, come home, eat dinner together, and go to bed on a reasonably similar timetable.

It's also important for you to remember that while it may be a family member who has an anxiety disorder, the recovery process is stressful for everybody. You should build your own support network of friends and family that you can rely on for support, and think about joining a support group of your own for family members of patients.

IF YOUR FRIEND IS THREATENING SUICIDE

Sometimes, symptoms of panic or a specific event, stress, or crisis—such as a bad grade, a breakup, or a death in the family—can trigger suicidal behavior in someone with an anxiety disorder. If someone you care about is talking about suicide or shows any warning signs of suicide, don't wait to see if he or she starts to feel better. Talk about it and report it to a responsible adult. Most of the time, people who are considering suicide are willing to discuss it if someone asks them out of concern and care. A tragic fact is that many kids contemplating suicide have told someone about their thoughts, but it wasn't reported until it was too late.

A friend may share with you that he or she is having suicidal thoughts. This can frighten you or make you feel uncomfortable. You might worry that talking to a friend about his or her thoughts of suicide or hurting themselves will somehow encourage the person to do so. If won't. It's always a good thing to talk to a friend about any suicidal thoughts. Just talking about suicidal thoughts may help your friend feel less alone and less isolated. Suicidal people often feel that no one really understands or cares, so showing them that you do can have an impact. You may be able to help your friend consider other solutions to his or her problems.

IF A FRIEND OR FAMILY MEMBER IS IN CRISIS

> ➤ Try to get the person to seek help immediately from an emergency room, physician, or mental health professional.
> ➤ If your friend is suicidal and won't get help, share your concerns with your parents, a trusted teacher or other adult, or the school nurse. Don't worry about whether your friend will be mad at you.

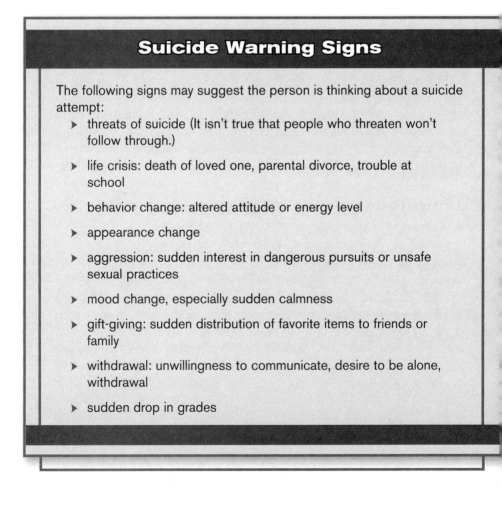

Suicide Warning Signs

The following signs may suggest the person is thinking about a suicide attempt:

> ➤ threats of suicide (It isn't true that people who threaten won't follow through.)
>
> ➤ life crisis: death of loved one, parental divorce, trouble at school
>
> ➤ behavior change: altered attitude or energy level
>
> ➤ appearance change
>
> ➤ aggression: sudden interest in dangerous pursuits or unsafe sexual practices
>
> ➤ mood change, especially sudden calmness
>
> ➤ gift-giving: sudden distribution of favorite items to friends or family
>
> ➤ withdrawal: unwillingness to communicate, desire to be alone, withdrawal
>
> ➤ sudden drop in grades

▶ Take seriously any comments about suicide or wishing to die. Even if you don't believe your family member or friend will actually attempt suicide, the person is clearly in distress and needs mental health treatment.

Sometimes, you may suspect your friend may be thinking about suicide, but what do you do if he or she hasn't come right out and shared these thoughts with you? It's not easy asking someone if he or she is having thoughts about suicide. You might try this: "I've noticed that you've been talking a lot about death. Have you been having thoughts about trying to kill yourself?"

If your friend shares thoughts of self-harm, try to listen without judgment. You may have a strong reaction to what he's saying, but try to avoid comments like "That's just silly!" or "That's stupid! Why would you want to do that?" Reassure your friend that you care and you're there to try to help. If you think your friend is in immediate danger, try to stay with him or her and make sure he or she isn't left alone.

A friend might try to swear you to secrecy before telling you about their suicidal thoughts. Being seen as a "rat" or a tattletale is something most kids want to avoid, and many kids may fear that telling someone else would be a betrayal. But in a life-or-death situation, you really have no choice. You need to share your concerns with an adult you trust as soon as possible. Ideally, that might be someone at school who can intervene for you. Although you may think you'll be able to help your friend by yourself, it's always safest to get help.

If necessary, call 911 or the toll-free number for a suicide crisis line (you can find local suicide crisis numbers listed in your phone book), or call the National Suicide Prevention Lifeline listed below.

National Suicide Prevention Lifeline

(800) 273-TALK or (800) 273-8255
TTY: (800) 799-4889

WHAT YOU NEED TO KNOW

> If you think that your friend's actions could result in serious harm, it's your responsibility as a friend to get help for that person.

> Don't be judgmental, tease, or trivialize the problem, and don't try to "fix" the person's anxiety.

> Be supportive; listen in a caring, nonjudgmental way; and make sure your friends know you're there to listen if they'd like to talk.

> If a family member has an anxiety disorder, learn as much as you can and work with a family therapist to learn how best to help your family member.

> Suicide warning signs include threats of suicide, a life crisis, behavior change, change in appearance, aggression, mood changes, sudden distribution of favorite items to friends or family, withdrawal, and sudden drop in grades.

> If someone talks about suicide or shows any warning signs of suicide, report it to a responsible adult right away.

> It's always a good thing to talk to a friend with suicidal thoughts, because this can help your friend feel less alone and less isolated.

Paying for Care

Kim was a 17-year-old college freshman struggling with various anxiety issues. Things got so bad that she decided to see a therapist, but money was an issue. Her dad had lost his job a year ago, and her mom's job barely covered the basics. The family couldn't afford health insurance, but they earned too much to qualify for state aid. Her family knew she needed help, but they just didn't know how they could afford it. Paying for mental health care is usually a problem for adults to solve, but many teens are aware of their family's financial problems. Friends might even confide that they want to see a therapist but their family just can't afford it. Counseling and medication costs combined with skyrocketing insurance premiums and dwindling coverage are making good mental health treatment an unreachable goal for many families. What can you do if your parents make too much money to qualify for Medicaid coverage but not enough to pay for your doctor visits, therapy, and medications?

Fortunately, there are ways to get the care you or a family member might need. Your parents can shop around for price and quality by asking for suggestions from people they trust. Different types of professionals charge different fees. In general, psychiatrists charge the highest fees and pastoral counselors charge the lowest. This doesn't mean that the most expensive treatment will always be the best or that the least expensive won't work. Community mental health agencies, some private mental health professionals, and some family service agencies charge fees based on a patient's ability to pay.

Community-based services. First, check into free community-based services. If your town has a community mental health center, it will offer a range of mental health treatment and counseling services at a reduced rate for low-income families. However, these centers usually require that you either have private insurance or that you are on welfare.

County services. Contact your county mental health department to find out what services are offered or to which services you can be referred. The cost of public services depends on your ability to pay. You should be able to find the department's telephone number in the county government section of your phone book.

School-based services. Your public school may work with local mental health agencies to identify problems and provide needed services.

Pastoral counseling. Certified pastoral counselors are ministers with advanced degrees in pastoral counseling, and they have professional counseling experience. This type of counseling is often available on a sliding-scale fee basis. That means that the less income your family has, the less you have to pay.

Medical insurance. If your family has medical insurance, look into therapists that are covered by your plan, or "in network." You might find, though, that the best therapists in your area are "out-of-network," which either raises your parents' out-of-pocket expense or means your policy won't cover the person at all. If possible, see if your family can pay for this person themselves rather than accepting a lower-quality expert your plan covers.

Low-Cost Health Care Clinics

The federal bureau of the Health Resources and Services Administration (HRSA) provides a nationwide directory of clinics offering low- or no-cost health care. For information, visit http://www.ask.hrsa.gov/pc.

Medicaid. Medicaid is a state-run public health program that covers mental health care and transportation to care for people who live in poverty and earn less than the program's maximum income limit. States are required to cover a core set of benefits, including hospital, outpatient, doctor services, and home health services. States can choose to cover services by psychologists and social workers and services provided in clinics. More information about eligibility requirements is available at local welfare and medical assistance offices. Check with your state Medicaid office to see precisely what is covered where you live and what the income limits are. You also can find information about Medicaid at http://www.CMS.gov.

MANAGED CARE

The idea of managing treatment services has become part of all types of public funding and insurance plans as a way of trying to keep costs down. Managed care means that the plan usually requires you to get approval from the managed care company before you go for treatment. After you've been treated for a while, the managed care company reviews how things are going and determines whether to pay for any more treatment. The idea behind this is to avoid paying for excess or unnecessary services.

If your parents have a managed care health insurance plan, you must get authorization from your managed care company before going for treatment. The company will authorize a limited number of sessions. Most managed care companies will approve well-known treatment techniques such as cognitive-behavioral therapy, so your parents shouldn't have trouble getting approval for such treatment for problems related to mild or serious anxiety.

EMPLOYEE ASSISTANCE PROGRAMS

Your parents' employers may offer an employee assistance program for their workers and their families. These special programs cover brief treatments for mental health problems that allow you to see a mental health professional for a number of free sessions (paid for by the employer) as a way to prevent small problems from becoming bigger ones. You and your parents should make sure that the professional you are referred to has the experience to deal with your particular type of problem.

MEDICATION COSTS

Many medications used to treat anxiety disorders are expensive. This doesn't mean you're out of luck if you don't have insurance or your plan doesn't include a prescription drug benefit. Drug companies give free samples of their drugs to doctors; many physicians will offer these samples to you free if you can't afford them. If your doctor doesn't offer, ask whether any samples are available.

Many people don't know this, but most drug companies also offer free medications to patients who can't afford them. These special programs, usually called patient assistance programs or indigent drug programs, typically require a doctor's consent, proof of financial status, and proof that your family has no health insurance or prescription drug benefits.

Patient assistance programs. Individual drug companies often list their programs online, but to make things easier, you can visit several Web sites (listed below) that have gathered information about many patient assistance programs providing free prescription medications to eligible participants.

NAMI Prescription Drug Patient Assistance Programs
http://www.nami.org/helpline/freemed.htm

NeedyMeds program
http://www.needymeds.com

RxOutreach
http://www.rxassist.org

The Medicine Program
http://www.themedicineprogram.com

Partnership for Prescription Assistance
https://www.pparx.org/Intro.php

Prescription Drug Assistance Programs
http://www.phrma.org

Canadian medications. Many people save money by ordering their medications from Canada, a move that has alarmed the U.S. government for safety concerns but that consumer advocates insist makes economic sense. If you choose this alternative, try to find a Web site that is as reputable as possible. Several states have developed programs for residents to buy medications from Canada:

▶ Illinois, Vermont, Wisconsin, Missouri, Kansas: Residents in these states can participate in I-SaveRx, a mail-order pharmacy program that is simple to use and could save you money. The program was developed by the governor of Illinois to pro-vide mail-order access to lower-cost brand prescription drugs from Canada, the United Kingdom, and Ireland. Visit http://www.i-saverx.net.

▶ Minnesota: The governor of this state has set up a Web site to help residents find less expensive drugs abroad. This Web site allows you to buy drugs from the United Kingdom. Contact Minnesota RxConnect at http://www.state.mn.us/portal/mn/jsp/home.do?agency = Rx.

▶ North Dakota: This state's Web page on Canadian drugs offers detailed explanations and links to Web sites to help you import medications. Visit http://www.governor.state.nd.us/prescriptiondrug.html.

WHAT YOU NEED TO KNOW

▶ Community mental health agencies, some private mental health professionals, and some family service agencies charge fees based on a patient's ability to pay.

▶ Community-based services offer a range of mental health treatment and counseling services at a reduced rate for low-income families.

▶ Affordable care may be provided by county mental health departments, school-based services, or a religious leader (pastoral counselor).

▶ Medicaid is a state-run public health program that may cover mental health care and transportation for people who live in poverty.

▶ Employee assistance programs for workers and their families cover brief treatments for mental health problems.

▶ Doctors may give you free samples of medications, and most drug companies also offer free medications to patients who can't afford them.

APPENDIX 1

Associations and Support Groups

The groups and organizations listed here are good sources to consider for aid or information. Note that addresses and Web site URLs are subject to change, but an Internet search of an association's name or key related terms can turn up new Web sites and additional resources. For some groups that emphasize their online presence, only Web site URLs are listed.

ADVOCACY

Federation of Families for Children's Mental Health
1101 King Street, Suite 420
Alexandria, VA 22314
(703) 684-7710
http://www.ffcmh.org
A nonprofit group working for mental health rights of children.

Mental Health Clients for Wellness & Recovery Inc. (MHCWAR)
1010 University Avenue
PMB #1661
San Diego, CA 92103
http://www.mhcwar.org
A nonprofit group of people with co-occurring conditions volunteering to empower each other and their communities. Located in California and organized by clients for clients, MHCWAR implements direct advocacy activities to empower mental health clients to advocate directly for regional health services programs and better mental health services.

National Mental Health Consumer's Self-Help Clearinghouse
1211 Chestnut Street, Suite 1207
Philadelphia, PA 19107
(800) 553-4539
info@mhselfhelp.org

http://www.mhselfhelp.org
A consumer-run national technical assistance center serving the mental health consumer movement. It helps connect individuals to self-help and advocacy resources and offers expertise to self-help groups and other peer-run services for mental health consumers.

ANXIETY DISORDERS
Anxieties.com
http://www.divepsych.com/
Web site featuring information about anxiety, a self-assessment questionnaire, self-help publications, workshops for professionals, e-mailed newsletters, and much more.

The Anxiety & Panic Internet Resource (TAPIR)
http://www.algy.com/anxiety/index.shtml
An Internet self-help resource for people with anxiety disorders, including panic attacks, phobias, extreme shyness, obsessive-compulsive behaviors, and generalized anxiety. TAPIR is a free grassroots Web site dedicated to providing information, relief, and support for those recovering from debilitating anxiety.

Anxiety Disorders Association of America (ADAA)
8730 Georgia Avenue, Suite 600
Silver Spring, MD 20910
(240) 485-1001
http://www.adaa.org
The ADAA promotes the prevention and cure of anxiety disorders and works to improve the lives of all people who suffer from them.

Anxiety Disorders Association of Canada
　　Association Canadienne des Troubles Anxieux
P.O. Box 461, Station "D"
Scarborough, Ontario M1R 5B8
CANADA
(888) 223-2252
contactus@anxietycanada.ca
http://www.anxietycanada.ca
This association was established in 2001 through the joint efforts of the Anxiety Disorders Associations of British Columbia, Manitoba, and Ontario and the Association/Troubles Anxieux du Québec to increase the awareness of anxiety disorders/conditions and related

conditions (depression, bipolar depression, and substance abuse) and their impact on people's lives across Canada.

Anxiety Treatment Network of Southwest Michigan
http://www.anxietytreatmentnetwork.org

A free resource for those with anxiety disorders in southwest Michigan, this includes an online newsletter; information about support groups, therapists, and presentations in this area; and book reviews and links to national organizations such as ADAA and Freedom From Fear. The network encourages the use of research-based approaches for the treatment and prevention of anxiety disorders.

Childhood Anxiety Network
3741 Locke Lane
Prospect, KY 40059
http://www.childhoodanxietynetwork.org

A professional and practical guide into the world of childhood anxiety and related childhood disorders, providing the newest research and information about OCD, panic, selective mutism, separation anxiety, generalized anxiety disorder (GAD), social anxiety, post-traumatic stress disorder (PTSD), trichotillomania, and specific phobia. The group's primary mission is to educate, promote public awareness, and advocate the early diagnosis of anxiety disorders.

ENcourage Connection
http://www.encourageconnection.com

ENcourage connection is the Web site portal for a message board (ENcourage Community) and newsletter (ENcourage Newsletter) for people working toward recovery from excessive anxiety, panic, and agoraphobia. ENcourage Community is a popular anxiety/ panic message board founded by the creators of ENcourage Newsletter, which began as a subscription publication eight years ago. ENcourage Web sites were created to be of interest to those working toward recovery from panic disorder and/or agoraphobia, as well as to treatment professionals in the field.

Freedom From Fear (FFF)
308 Seaview Avenue
Staten Island, NY 10305
(718) 351-1717 (ext. 24)
http://www.freedomfromfear.com

This national not-for-profit mental health advocacy association's mission is to aid and counsel individuals who suffer from anxiety and depressive illnesses and their families. It was founded in 1984 by Mary Guardino, who established FFF as an outgrowth of her own personal experiences of suffering with anxiety and depressive illnesses for more than 25 years.

International Association of Anxiety Management
http://www.anxman.org/contact.asp
The definitive Web resource for sufferers of anxiety disorders, phobias, and panic. The Web site is filled with information on all types of anxiety disorders, tips for coping, links to research, FAQs about anxiety, anxiety assessment, and much more.

National Anxiety Foundation
3135 Custer Drive
Lexington, KY 40517
http://www.lexington-on-line.com/naf.html

Psychological Self-Help
http://mentalhelp.net/psyhelp
Psychological Self-Help is a free online Web site that covers all kinds of problems in the anxiety area, including trauma, stress, anxiety, fears, worry, shyness, obsession-compulsions, and various health and pain disorders.

BEHAVIOR THERAPY
The Association for Behavioral and Cognitive Therapies
305 7th Avenue, 16th Floor
New York, NY 10001
(212) 647-1890
http://www.aabt.org
A professional interdisciplinary organization concerned with the application of behavioral and cognitive sciences to understanding human behavior, developing interventions to enhance the human condition, and promoting the appropriate use of these interventions.

The British Association for Behavioural and Cognitive Psychotherapies (BABCP)
Victoria Buildings
9-13 Silver Street
Bury, BL9 OEU
0161-797-4484

http://www.babcp.com
A multidisciplinary interest group for professionals involved in the
  practice and theory of behavioral and cognitive psychotherapy.

COGNITIVE THERAPY
Academy of Cognitive Therapy
(610) 664-1273
info@academyofct.org
http://www.academyofct.org
The only certifying organization for cognitive-behavioral therapy
  that evaluates applicants' knowledge and ability before granting
  certification. A nonprofit organization founded in 1999 by a group
  of clinicians, educators, and researchers in the field of cognitive
  therapy, the academy supports continuing education and research
  in cognitive therapy, provides information about cognitive therapy
  for professionals and the public, and actively works toward the
  identification and certification of clinicians skilled in cognitive
  therapy. The standards of the academy are designed to identify
  clinicians with the necessary training, experience, and knowledge
  to be effective cognitive therapists. Lack of rigor in certification
  represents a significant problem for both clinicians and consumers.
  Certification by the Academy of Cognitive Therapy indicates to
  the public, potential employers, and other clinicians that the
  individual is a skilled cognitive therapist. The academy includes
  physicians, psychologists, social workers, and other mental health
  professionals from around the world.

The International Association for Cognitive Psychotherapy (IACP)
http://www.cognitivetherapyassociation.org
A professional, scientific, interdisciplinary organization whose
  mission is to encourage the growth of cognitive psychotherapy as
  a professional activity and scientific discipline. In addition, the
  association serves as a resource and information center for matters
  related to cognitive psychotherapy.

DEPRESSION
Depression and Related Affective Disorders Association (DRADA)
2330 West Joppa Road, Suite 100
Lutherville, MD 21093
(410) 583-2919
drada@jhmi.edu
http://www.drada.org

A community organization that serves individuals who are affected by a depressive illness and their families, health care professionals, and the general public. The association provides assistance to self-help groups, provides education and information, and lends support to research programs. DRADA understands the need to eliminate the stigma that is attached to mood disorders and strives to promote public knowledge of depression signs and symptoms as well as resources available to people affected by these illnesses.

National Foundation for Depressive Illness, Inc.
P.O. Box 2257
New York, NY 10116
(800) 239-1265
http://www.depression.org
A nonprofit organization working to support individuals with depression, providing information, resources, and details on research.

FAMILY SUPPORT
Family Resource Center on Disabilities (FRCD)
20 East Jackson Boulevard, Room 900
Chicago, IL 60604
(800) 952-4199 (Voice/TTY; toll-free in IL only)
(312) 939-3513
(312) 939-3519 (TTY)
http://www.frcd.org
A coalition of parents and professional organizations organized in 1969 by parents, professionals, and volunteers wanting to improve services for all children with disabilities. In one year FRCD answers more than 8,000 telephone and mail requests for information and assistance. During its 30-year existence FRCD has answered more than 200,000 requests for information, training, and support services.

Federation of Families for Children's Mental Health
1021 Prince Street
Alexandria, VA 22314-2971
ffcmh@ffcmh.com
http://www.ffcmh.org
This national family-run organization is dedicated exclusively to helping children with mental health needs and their families

achieve a better quality of life. The group helps policy makers, agencies, and providers become more effective in delivering support and services that foster healthy emotional development for all children.

Research and Training Center on Family Support and Children's Mental Health
Portland State University
P.O. Box 751
Portland, OR 97207-0751
(800) 628-1696
(503) 725-4040
(503) 725-4165 (TTY)
caplane@rri.pdx.edu
http://www.rtc.pdx.edu
This research center is dedicated to promoting effective services for families and their children with emotional, behavioral, or mental health disorders.

FEARS
Freedom From Fear (FFF)
308 Seaview Avenue
Staten Island, NY 10305
(718) 351-1717 (ext. 24)
help@freedomfromfear.org
http://www.freedomfromfear.org
A national nonprofit mental health advocacy association whose mission is to improve the lives of all those affected by anxiety, depressive, and related disorders through advocacy, education, research, and community support. The online FFF has developed an anxiety and depression screening program with a free consultation from a health care professional.

GENERALIZED ANXIETY DISORDER
UCLA Child OCD, Anxiety, and Tic Disorders Program Homepage
http://www.npi.ucla.edu/caap
Web site with information, resources, studies, and more about OCD, selective mutism, social phobia, GAD, separation anxiety disorder, tic disorders, and trichotillomania.

GOVERNMENT ORGANIZATIONS
Food and Drug Administration
5600 Fishers Lane
Rockville, MD 20857
(301) 472-4750
http://www.fda.gov
The FDA regulates drugs and medical devices to ensure that they are safe and effective and provides a number of publications for consumers.

HRSA Information Center
Parklawn Building
5600 Fishers Lane
Rockville, MD 20857
(888) 275-4772
http://www.ask.hrsa.gov
Provides publications and resources on health care services for low-income, uninsured individuals and those with special health care needs.

National Information Center for Children and Youth with Disabilities
P.O. Box 1492
Washington, DC 20013-1492
(800) 695-0285
http://www.nichcy.org
This national information and referral clearinghouse on special education and disability-related issues provides information about local, state, and national disability groups and gives technical assistance to parents and professionals.

National Institute of Child Health and Human Development
Building 31, Room 2A32
9000 Rockville Pike
Bethesda, MD 20892-2425
(301) 496-5133
http://www.nichd.nih.gov
Supports research into the health of children and offers information on a wide variety of topics relevant to children and maternal health.

National Institute of Mental Health (NIMH)
5600 Fisher Lane
Rockville, MD 20857

(301) 443-4513

http://www.nimh.nih.gov

One of 27 components of the National Institutes of Health and the
federal government's principal biomedical and behavioral research
agency, this is the foremost mental health research organization
in the world. Its mission is to reduce the burden of mental illness
and behavioral disorders through research on mind, brain, and
behavior. NIMH is also committed to educating the public about
mental disorders and has developed many booklets and fact
sheets that provide the latest research-based information on
these illnesses. Its Web site provides information to the public,
researchers, and clinicians on a range of mental disorders affecting
adults and children, including anxiety disorders. There are also
links to other federal government Web sites and resources, such as
the Surgeon General's Report on Mental Health.

National Mental Health Information Center

P.O. Box 42557

Washington, DC 20013-1133

(800) 789-2647

info@mentalhealth.org

http://www.mentalhealth.samhsa.gov

A federal health information referral service that puts consumers who
have mental health questions in touch with organizations that are
best able to provide answers. This organization also can provide
help with financial issues.

MENTAL HEALTH

Center for Mental Health Services

5600 Fishers Lane, Room 17-99

Rockville, MD 20857

http://www.mentalhealth.org

Federal agency that provides information and resources on mental
health, including a database of community resources, an extensive
catalog, events, and more. The goal of this agency is to provide
the treatment and support services needed by adults with mental
disorders and children with serious emotional problems.

National Council for Community Behavioral Health Care

12300 Twinbrook Parkway, Suite 320

Rockville, MD 20852

http://www.nccbh.org

A nonprofit group working to enhance community mental health care centers.

National Mental Health Consumer's Self-Help Clearinghouse
1211 Chestnut Street, Suite 1207
Philadelphia, PA 19107
(800) 553-4539
info@mhselfhelp.org
http://www.mhselfhelp.org
A consumer-run national technical assistance center serving the mental health consumer movement. The organization helps connect individuals to self-help and advocacy resources and offers expertise to self-help groups and other peer-run services for mental health consumers.

MENTAL ILLNESS
National Alliance on Mental Illness (NAMI)
Colonial Place Three
2107 Wilson Boulevard, Suite 300
Arlington, VA 22201-3042
(800) 950-6264
(703) 524-7600
(703) 516-7991 (TTY)
http://www.nami.org
A nonprofit, grassroots, self-help, support, and advocacy organization of consumers, families, and friends of people with severe mental illnesses, such as schizophrenia, major depression, bipolar disorder, obsessive-compulsive disorder, and anxiety disorders, dedicated to support individuals with mental illness and their families.

National Association for the Dually Diagnosed (NADD)
132 Fair Street
Kingston, NY 12401
(800) 331-5362
(845) 331-4336
http://www.thenadd.org
Nonprofit organization to support those with both mental illness and mental retardation.

OBSESSIVE-COMPULSIVE DISORDER
Obsessive-Compulsive Foundation, Inc. (OCF)
676 State Street
New Haven, CT 06511
(203) 401-2070

info@ocfoundation.org
http://www.ocfoundation.org
The Obsessive-Compulsive Foundation (OCF) is an international not-for-profit organization composed of people with obsessive-compulsive disorder (OCD) and related disorders, their families and friends, professionals, and other concerned individuals. Founded by a group of individuals with OCD in 1986, the group's mission is to educate the public and professional communities about OCD and related disorders, to provide assistance to individuals with OCD and related disorders and their family and friends, and to support research into the causes and effective treatments of OCD and related disorders.

UCLA Child OCD, Anxiety, and Tic Disorders
Program Homepage
http://www.npi.ucla.edu/caap
Web site with information, resources, studies, and more about OCD, selective mutism, social phobia, GAD, separation anxiety disorder, tic disorders, and trichotillomania.

PANIC
The Anxiety & Panic Internet Resource (TAPIR)
http://www.algy.com/anxiety/index.shtml
An Internet resource for people with anxiety disorders, including panic attacks, phobias, extreme shyness, obsessive-compulsive behaviors, and generalized anxiety. TAPIR is a free grassroots Web site dedicated to providing information, relief, and support for those recovering from debilitating anxiety.

ENcourage Connection
http://www.encourageconnection.com/
*The Web site portal for a message board (*ENcourage Community*) and newsletter (*ENcourage Newsletter*) *for people working toward recovery from excessive anxiety, panic, and agoraphobia. ENcourage Community is a popular anxiety/panic message board founded by the creators of* ENcourage Newsletter, *which began as a subscription publication eight years ago. ENcourage Web sites were created to be of interest to those working toward recovery from panic disorder and/or agoraphobia, as well as to treatment professionals in the field.*

The Panic Center
http://www.paniccenter.net

An interactive Web site dedicated to helping those who suffer from panic disorder, dedicated to promoting interaction between panic sufferers and health care professionals.

Panic in Scuba Divers
http://www.divepsych.com
Web site hosted by Dr. David F. Colvard, diplomate of the American Board of Psychiatry and Neurology and member of the Underwater & Hyperbaric Medical Society. Information for divers with panic or anxiety issues, including studies and surveys of natural disasters and diving, information and studies on PTSD, and many links.

PHOBIAS (*See also* SOCIAL PHOBIA)
ABIL: Agoraphobics Building Independent Lives
2501 Fox Harbor Court
Richmond, VA 23235-2829
(804) 353-3964
answers@anxietysupport.org
http://www.anxietysupport.org/b001menu.htm
A national network for anxiety support and education, headquartered in Richmond, Virginia, that provides hope, support, and advocacy for people suffering from debilitating phobias, panic attacks, and/or agoraphobia. Its Web site offers information, education, self-help, support, and seminars on anxiety issues. The group works to facilitate the development of self-help groups and establish a national network for persons with panic disorders; provides advocacy and information on rights-related issues; develops a strong link with the professional community to improve the quality of treatment; disseminates current information to members, professionals, and the general public; and works to eliminate the stigma associated with panic disorder.

Anxiety Disorders Association of America (ADAA)
11900 Parklawn Drive #100
Rockville, MD 20852-2624
(301) 231-9350
AnxDis@aol.com
http://www.adaa.org
The ADAA promotes the prevention and cure of anxiety disorders and works to improve the lives of all people who suffer from them.

Childhood Anxiety Network

3741 Locke Lane

Prospect, KY 40059

http://www.childhoodanxietynetwork.org

A professional and practical guide into the world of childhood anxiety and related childhood disorders, providing the newest research and information about OCD, panic, selective mutism, separation anxiety, generalized anxiety disorder (GAD), social anxiety, post-traumatic stress disorder (PTSD), trichotillomania, and specific phobia. The group's primary mission is to educate, promote public awareness, and advocate the early diagnosis of anxiety disorders.

Dental Fear Central: Dental Phobia and Dental Anxiety Info

http://www.dentalfearcentral.com

Dental Fear Central is a free, nonprofit guide to dental phobia. Most people with a dental phobia feel utterly alone in their fear. Knowing that others have suffered the same way and have overcome or at least managed their fear of the dentist can be a great help. At this Web site, you'll also find practical advice on many of the issues surrounding dental phobias.

ENcourage Connection

http://www.encourageconnection.com

ENcourage connection is the Web site portal for a message board (ENcourage Community) and newsletter (ENcourage Newsletter) *for people working toward recovery from excessive anxiety, panic, and agoraphobia. ENcourage Community is a popular anxiety/ panic message board founded by the creators of* ENcourage Newsletter, *which began as a subscription publication eight years ago. ENcourage Web sites were created to be of interest to those working toward recovery from panic disorder and/or agoraphobia, as well as to treatment professionals in the field.*

National Phobics Society (NPS)

Zion Community Resource Centre

339 Stretford Road

Hulme

Manchester, M15 4ZY

Great Britain

0870 122 2325

http://www.phobics-society.org.uk

*NPS was established in 1970, and over the years it has grown to
become the largest charity dealing with anxiety and phobias. The
society can provide support and help if you've been diagnosed
with or suspect you may have an anxiety condition. The society
also can help you deal with specific phobias, such as fear of
spiders, blushing, vomiting, being alone, public speaking, heights,
or any fear that's stopped you from getting on with your life.*

POST-TRAUMATIC STRESS DISORDER (PTSD)
American Academy of Experts in Traumatic Stress
368 Veterans Memorial Highway
Commack, NY 11725
(631) 543-2217
info@aaets.org
http://www.aaets.org/abtaaets.htm
*The Academy's mission is to increase awareness of the effects
of traumatic events and, ultimately, to improve the quality of
intervention with survivors.*

Anxiety Disorders Association of America (ADAA)
11900 Parklawn Drive #100
Rockville, MD 20852-2624
(301) 231-9350
AnxDis@aol.com
http://www.adaa.org
*The ADAA promotes the prevention and cure of anxiety disorders
and works to improve the lives of all people who suffer from them.*

The Association of Traumatic Stress Specialists (ATSS)
P.O. Box 246
Phillips, ME 04966
(800) 991-ATSS
(800) 991-2877
http://www.atss.info
*The Association of Traumatic Stress Specialists is a nonprofit
membership organization for developing standards of service and
education for those who provide such critical emotional care to
trauma victims and survivors. ATSS is dedicated to excellence
in training, education, and experience to ensure that victims
of crime, abuse, war, terrorism, and disasters receive the most
compassionate and effective care possible.*

Gift from Within
16 Cobb Hill Road
Camden, ME 04843
(207) 236-8858
(207) 236-2818 (fax)
http://www.giftfromwithin.org
A nonprofit organization dedicated to those who suffer post-traumatic stress disorder (PTSD), those at risk for PTSD, and those who care for traumatized individuals. The group develops and disseminates educational material, including videotapes, articles, books, and other resources, through its Web site and maintains a roster of survivors who are willing to participate in an international network of peer support. At least 10,000,000 Americans have experienced some form of PTSD.

International Society for Traumatic Stress Studies
60 Revere Drive, Suite 500
Northbrook, IL 60062
(847) 480-9028
istss@istss.org
http://www.istss.org
Nonprofit group dedicated to providing information about studies that seek to reduce traumatic stress and its immediate and long-term consequences. Members of ISTSS include psychiatrists, psychologists, social workers, nurses, counselors, researchers, administrators, advocates, journalists, clergy, and others with an interest in the study and treatment of traumatic stress.

National Center for PTSD
VA Medical Center (116D)
215 North Main Street
White River Junction, VT 05009
(802) 296-6300
http://www.ncptsd.org
The National Center for Post-Traumatic Stress Disorder (PTSD) was created within the Department of Veterans Affairs in 1989, in response to a congressional mandate to address the needs of veterans with military-related PTSD. Its mission is to advance the clinical care and social welfare of America's veterans through research, education, and training in the science, diagnosis, and treatment of PTSD and stress-related disorders.

National Child Traumatic Stress Network (NCTSN)
http://www.nctsnet.org/nccts/nav.do?pid = ctr_main
The mission of the NCTSN is to raise the standard of care and
improve access to services for traumatized children, their families,
and their communities throughout the United States. The Web
site offers a resource center with tips on finding help and lots of
helpful basic information.

PTSD Alliance
(877) 507-PTSD
http://www.ptsdalliance.org/home2.html
A group of professional and advocacy organizations that have
joined forces to provide educational resources to individuals
diagnosed with PTSD and their loved ones, to those at risk
for developing PTSD, and to medical, health care, and other
professionals.

SIDRAN—Sidran Traumatic Stress Foundation
200 E. Joppa Road, Suite 207
Baltimore, MD 21286
(410) 825-8888
http://www.sidran.org
A national nonprofit organization devoted to education, advocacy,
and research related to the early recognition and treatment of
traumatic stress and trauma-generated disorders.

PROFESSIONAL ASSOCIATIONS

The American Academy of Child and Adolescent Psychiatry
(AACAP)
3615 Wisconsin Avenue, NW
Washington, DC 20016-3007
(202) 966-7300
http://www.aacap.org
The leading national nonprofit professional medical association
dedicated to treating and improving the quality of life for children,
adolescents, and families affected by mental disorders. Established
in 1953, its members actively research, evaluate, diagnose,
and treat psychiatric disorders. The AACAP widely distributes
information on mental illnesses, advances efforts in the prevention
of mental illnesses, and ensures proper treatment and access to
services for children and adolescents.

American Academy of Experts in Traumatic Stress
368 Veterans Memorial Highway
Commack, NY 11725
(631) 543-2217
info@aaets.org
http://www.aaets.org/abtaaets.htm
The Academy's mission is to increase awareness of the effects
of traumatic events and, ultimately, to improve the quality of
intervention with survivors.

American Academy of Pediatrics (AAP)
141 Northwest Point Boulevard
Elk Grove Village, IL 60007-1098
(847) 434-4000
http://www.aap.org
The leading national nonprofit professional medical association
dedicated to treating and improving the quality of life for children
and adolescents, this organization of 60,000 pediatricians is
committed to attaining the best physical, mental, and social health
for all infants, children, teens, and young adults.

American Association of Pastoral Counselors (AAPC)
9504-A Lee Highway
Fairfax, VA 22031
(703) 385-6967
info@aapc.org
http://www.aapc.org
The American Association of Pastoral Counselors (AAPC)
sets professional standards for more than 3,000 pastoral
counselors and 100 pastoral counseling centers in North
America and around the world. AAPC was founded in 1963
as an organization that certifies pastoral counselors, accredits
pastoral counseling centers, and approves training programs.
It is nonsectarian and respects the spiritual commitments
and religious traditions of those who seek assistance without
imposing counselor beliefs onto the client.

American Psychiatric Association (APA)
1000 Wilson Boulevard, Suite 1825
Arlington, VA 22209-3901
(703) 907-7300
http://www.psych.org

*The American Psychiatric Association is a medical specialty
society recognized worldwide with more than 35,000 U.S. and
international member physicians who work together to ensure
humane care and effective treatment for all people. Its vision is
a society that has available and accessible quality psychiatric
diagnosis and treatment. The APA is an organization composed
primarily of medical specialists who are qualified, or in the process
of becoming qualified, as psychiatrists.*

American Psychological Association (APA)
750 First Street, NE
Washington, DC 20002-4242
(800) 374-2721
(202) 336-5510
http://www.apa.org

*Based in Washington, D.C., APA is a scientific and professional
organization that represents psychology in the United States.
With 150,000 members, the APA is the largest association
of psychologists worldwide. The American Psychological
Association tries to advance psychology as a science and
profession and as a means of promoting health, education,
and human welfare.*

The Association of Traumatic Stress Specialists (ATSS)
P.O. Box 246
Phillips, ME 04966
(800) 991-ATSS
(800) 991-2877
http://www.atss.info

*The Association of Traumatic Stress Specialists is a nonprofit
membership organization for developing standards of service and
education for those who provide such critical emotional care to
trauma victims and survivors. The ATSS is dedicated to excellence
in training, education, and experience to ensure that victims
of crime, abuse, war, terrorism, and disasters receive the most
compassionate and effective care possible.*

SELECTIVE MUTISM
Selective Mutism Foundation
P.O. Box 13133
Sissonville, WV 25360-0133
http://www.selectivemutismfoundation.org

*Nonprofit organization founded to further research, advocacy, social
acceptance, and the understanding of selective mutism as a
debilitating disorder.*

Selective Mutism Group—Childhood Anxiety Disorders Network (SMG-CAN)

http://www.selectivemutism.org

*SMG-CAN is a division of the charitable not-for-profit organization
the Childhood Anxiety Network, Inc. This group has formed a
community to help others by sharing experiences and knowledge,
fulfilling a mission to promote public awareness, to research and
educate about selective mutism, and to speak out for the children
who can't speak for themselves.*

UCLA Child OCD, Anxiety, and Tic Disorders Program Homepage

http://www.npi.ucla.edu/caap

*Web site with information, resources, studies, and more about OCD,
selective mutism, social phobia, GAD, separation anxiety disorder,
tic disorders, and trichotillomania.*

SOCIAL ANXIETY/SOCIAL PHOBIA

Social Phobia/Social Anxiety Association (SP/SAA)

http://www.socialphobia.org/mission.html#mission1

*A nonprofit organization officially organized in 1997 to meet the
growing needs of people throughout the world who have social
phobia or social anxiety. Membership in SP/SAA is open to anyone
interested in social anxiety disorder and in cooperating to help,
encourage, and support others.*

UCLA Child OCD, Anxiety, and Tic Disorders Program Homepage

http://www.npi.ucla.edu/caap

*Web site with information, resources, studies, and more about OCD,
selective mutism, social phobia, GAD, separation anxiety disorder,
tic disorders, and trichotillomania.*

SUICIDE

American Association of Suicidology (AAS)

5221 Wisconsin Avenue, NW
Washington, DC 20015
(202) 237-2280
http://www.suicidology.org

The goal of the American Association of Suicidology is to understand and prevent suicide. The organization provides information on current research, prevention, ways to help a suicidal person, and surviving suicide. Founded in 1968 by Edwin S. Shneidman, Ph.D., AAS promotes research, public awareness programs, public education, and training for professionals and volunteers. In addition, the AAS serves as a national clearinghouse for information on suicide. The membership of the AAS includes mental health and public health professionals, researchers, suicide prevention and crisis intervention centers, school districts, crisis center volunteers, survivors of suicide and a variety of laypersons who have an interest in suicide prevention. A list of crisis centers is available.

The American Foundation for Suicide Prevention (AFSP)
120 Wall Street, 22nd Floor
New York, NY 10005
(888) 333-AFSP
(212) 363-3500
http://www.afsp.org
The American Foundation for Suicide Prevention is the only national not-for-profit organization exclusively dedicated to funding research, developing prevention initiatives, and offering educational programs and conferences for survivors, mental health professionals, physicians, and the public. The foundation supports research projects that help further the understanding and treatment of depression and the prevention of suicide; provides information and education about suicide; promotes professional education for the recognition and treatment of depressed and suicidal individuals; publicizes the magnitude of the problems of depression and suicide and the need for research, prevention, and treatment; and supports programs for suicide survivor treatment, research, and education. The Web site offers links to other suicide and mental health sites.

Boys Town
14100 Crawford Street
Boys Town, NE 68010
(402) 498-1300 (8 AM to 5 PM CST Monday through Friday)
(800) 448-3000 (crisis hotline)
(800) 545-5771
http://www.boystown.org
Boys Town cares for troubled teens and for families in crisis. The hotline staff is trained to handle calls and questions about violence

and suicide. Girls and Boys Town, the original Father Flanagan's Boys' Home, is a leader in the treatment and care of abused, abandoned, and neglected girls and boys. Throughout its 88-year history, the nonprofit, nonsectarian organization has provided these children with a safe, caring, loving environment where they gain confidence to get better and learn skills to become productive citizens. Girls and Boys Town alumni and alumnae have gone on to become successful in all facets of life. Under the direction of Father Steven Boes, Girls and Boys Town cares for thousands of children and families each year from programs located at 19 sites in 15 states and the District of Columbia. Girls and Boys Town's National Headquarters and largest child-care facility are located at the world-famous historic Village of Boys Town in Nebraska.

Canadian Association for Suicide Prevention (CASP)
c/o The Support Network
301 11456 Jasper Avenue
Edmonton, Alberta T5K 0M1
CANADA
(780) 482-0198
casp@suiucideprevention.ca
http://www.casp-acps.ca
Web site for the CASP with information and links to suicide prevention in Canada.

Friends and Families of Suicide
http://www.friendsandfamiliesofsuicide.com
Web site featuring discussions, photo pages, retreats, chat rooms, and personal stories of family loss through suicide.

The Samaritans of New York
P.O. Box 1259
Madison Square Station
New York, NY 10159
(212) 673-3000
http://www.samaritansnyc.org
The Samaritans of New York is the local branch of the international humanitarian movement with more than 400 branches in 32 countries. A nonreligious, nonprofit organization, Samaritans is devoted to helping people who are in crisis and feeling suicidal through its volunteer-run programs that practice a communications-based response they call "befriending." This emphasizes listening to what a person in crisis is feeling and

*thinking without expressing personal judgments or opinions. Its
suicide prevention hotline operates 24 hours, seven days a week.
Staffed by more than 100 volunteers who go through intensive
training, it is the city's only confidential 24-hour hotline devoted
to preventing suicide. The hotline responds to callers from every
walk of life, with all kinds of problems. The Samaritans is
completely confidential and has no political, social, or cultural
agenda. Its sole purpose is to provide support to individuals and
groups who are in crisis, have lost someone to suicide, and/or
are feeling suicidal. Samaritans volunteers are caring individuals
of every age and walk of life who donate more than 20 hours a
month of their time.*

The Sibling Connection
http://www.counselingstlouis.net
*A Web site created as a resource for anyone who has experienced the
death or suicide of a brother or sister, adults who grew up with
a sibling who had a chronic and fatal disease, and professional
counselors, psychologists, therapists, and other health care providers.*

Yellow Ribbon International
P.O. Box 644
Westminster, CO 80036-0644
(303) 429-3530
ask4help@yellowribbon.org
http://www.yellowribbon.org
*The Yellow Ribbon program was founded in 1994 by the parents of Mike
Emme, a teenager who took his life when he did not know how to
let someone know he was in trouble and needed help. The program
provides yellow ribbon cards with the phone number of a national
suicide hotline and instructions on how to help a suicidal teen.*

TRICHOTILLOMANIA
Trichotillomania Learning Center, Inc.
303 Potrero #51
Santa Cruz, CA 95060
(831) 457-1004
http://www.trich.org/home/default.asp
*A national nonprofit organization established to provide information,
support, and referral sources regarding the experience and
treatment of trichotillomania (compulsive hair pulling). TLC's
educational resources are available to people with TTM, their*

family members and friends, therapeutic professionals, educators, and anyone with an interest in the subject. TLC's mission is to raise public awareness, to maintain a support network and treatment referral base, and to raise funds for research to find a cure for trichotillomania.

APPENDIX 2

Anxiety Screening Tools

One of the easiest ways to figure out if you have symptoms of an anxiety disorder is to take a screening test, which can help you recognize the signs. These tests aren't intended to provide a conclusive diagnosis or replace a proper evaluation by a physician or mental health professional. A positive result from any of the screening tools only indicates that you could benefit from a comprehensive mental health exam.

The Anxiety Disorders Association of America offers a variety of self-tests on its Web sites, as listed below. The ADAA does not have access to your answers and captures no information from these questionnaires.

Anxiety Disorder in Adolescents: A Self-Test
http://www.adaa.org/Public/selftest_ADA.htm

Anxiety Disorders: Self-Test for Family Members
http://www.adaa.org/Public/selftest_Family.htm

Generalized Anxiety Disorder Self-Test
http://www.adaa.org/Public/selftest_GAD.htm

OCD Self-Test
http://www.adaa.org/Public/selftest_OCD.htm

Panic Disorder Self-Test
http://www.adaa.org/Public/selftest_Panic.htm

Phobia Self-Test
http://www.adaa.org/Public/selftest_specialpho.htm

Post-Traumatic Stress Disorder Self-Test
http://www.adaa.org/Public/selftest_PTSD.htm

Social Phobia Self-Test
http://www.adaa.org/Public/selftest_socialpho.htm

APPENDIX 3

Phobias Listed by Fear

anger	angrophobia
animals	zoophobia
bees	apiphobia, melissophobia
birds	ornithophobia
blood	hemophobia or hematophobia
blushing	ereuthrophobia
bugs	acarophobia
cats	ailurophobia, elurophobia, felinophobia, galeophobia, gatophobia
contamination with dirt or germs	misophobia, mysophobia
darkness	achluophobia, myctophobia
dentists	dentophobia
disease	pathophobia
dogs	cynophobia
dreams	oneirophobia
enclosed or confined spaces	claustrophobia
fire	pyrophobia
floods	antlophobia
flying	aerophobia, aviophobia, aviatophobia, pteromerhanophobia

foreigners	xenophobia
fur or animal skins	doraphobia
ghosts	phasmophobia
heights	acrophobia, altophobia, batophobia, hypsiphobia
holy things	hagiophobia
injections	belonephobia, trypanophobia, needlephobia
insanity	agateophobia
itching	acarophobia
kidney disease	albuminurophobia
men	androphobia, arrhenphobia
microbes	bacillophobia
moving or making changes	tropophobia
noise	acousticophobia
numbers	arithmophobia
open high places	aeroacrophobia
open spaces	agoraphobia
opposite sex	heterophobia
pain	agliophobia
rabies	cynophobia, hydrophobophobia
saints	hagiophobia
scratches	amychophobia
sexual abuse	agraphobia
snakes	ophidiophobia
space	astrophobia

spiders	arachnophobia
teasing	catagelophobia
wasps	spheksophobia
water	hydrophobia
wild animals	agrizoophobia
writing in public	scriptophobia

GLOSSARY

acarophobia   Fear of itching or of bugs that cause itching.

achluophobia (also nyctaphobia)   Fear of darkness.

acrophobia (also altophobia, batophobia, hypsiphobia)   Fear of heights.

acousticophobia   Fear of noise.

aeroacrophobia   Fear of open high places.

aerophobia   Fear of airborne noxious substances, of drafts, or of swallowing air; also fear of flying.

affective disorder   A term that includes all mood disorders, including depression and bipolar depression.

agateophobia   Fear of insanity.

agliophobia   Fear of pain.

agoraphobia   A symptom of an anxiety disorder characterized by severe, pervasive anxiety about being in situations from which escape might be difficult or from which help may not be available in the event of a panic attack. People with agoraphobia fear crowded or confined situations where anxiety may escalate into panic attacks. As a result, people with agoraphobia often are confined to their homes.

agraphobia   Fear of sexual abuse.

agrizoophobia   Fear of wild animals.

ailurophobia (also elurophobia, felinophobia, galephobia, gatophobia)   Fear of cats.

albuminurophobia   Fear of kidney disease.

alprazolam (Xanax)   A benzodiazepine medication used to treat anxiety and panic disorder.

altophobia   See ACROPHOBIA.

amychophobia   Fear of scratches or of being scratched.

amygdala   A small region of the brain that experts believe is very important in the fear response, in emotions, and in anxiety.

Anafranil   See CLOMIPRAMINE.

androphobia (also arrhenphobia)   Fear of men.

anticholinergic   A group of common side effects typically caused by an older group of antidepressants, including dry mouth, constipation, urination problems, and blurry vision.

anticipatory anxiety   The fear of fear or fear of having an anxiety attack.

antidepressant   A medication used to treat depression and sometimes to treat anxiety disorders as well. Antidepressants include selective serotonin reuptake inhibitors (SSRIs), tricyclic antidepressants, and monoamine oxidase inhibitors (MAOIs).

antlophobia   Fear of floods.

anxiety   A sense of apprehension and fear often characterized by symptoms such as sweating, tension, and pounding heart.

anxiety attack   Another term for panic attack, an intense episode of extremely uncomfortable anxiety.

anxiety disorders   A group of disorders characterized by irrational and disabling fear or anxiety, including obsessive-compulsive disorder, panic disorder, social phobia, specific phobia, post-traumatic stress disorder, and generalized anxiety disorder.

anxiolytics   Antianxiety medications.

apiphobia (also melissophobia)   Fear of bees.

arachnophobia   The fear of spiders.

arithmophobia   Fear of numbers.

arrhenphobia   See ANDROPHOBIA.

astrophobia   Fear of space.

automatic thoughts   Thoughts or beliefs about everyday activities that occur so quickly a person must focus to recognize them.

autophobia   Fear of being alone or of oneself.

aversion therapy   A type of behavior therapy in which punishment or negative stimulation is used to eliminate undesired responses.

aviatophobia (also aerophobia, aviophobia, pteromerhanophobia)   Fear of flying.

aviophobia   See AVIATOPHOBIA.

avoidance conditioning   A form of learning in which a person is conditioned to avoid situations or places in order to avoid a negative consequence (such as anxiety).

bacillophobia   Fear of microbes.

batophobia   See ACROPHOBIA.

battle fatigue   An obsolete name for post-traumatic stress disorder.

behavior modification   Techniques based on learning theory that use reinforcers to change a person's behavior.

behavior therapy   A type of psychotherapy treatment used to eliminate undesirable behaviors and replace them with desirable ones by use of reinforcement and conditioning.

belonephobia (also needlephobia)   Fear of injections.

benzodiazepines   A class of drugs that act as tranquilizers, which may be used to treat some symptoms of some anxiety disorders.

beta blockers   A class of drugs used to lower blood pressure and that also may lessen physical symptoms of anxiety.

biofeedback   A therapy technique in which a person is taught to control body processes not normally considered to be under voluntary control, such as heart rate or skin temperature.

brief psychotherapy   Short-term therapy of eight to 12 sessions.

buproprion (Wellbutrin)   An antidepressant also used to treat social phobia, among other problems.

BuSpar   See BUSPIRONE.

buspirone (BuSpar)   An antianxiety drug prescribed primarily for generalized anxiety disorder.

caffeine   A chemical found in many drinks and foods that can trigger restlessness, nervousness, insomnia, twitching, stomach upset, and intoxication and that can worsen symptoms of anxiety disorders.

catagelophobia   Fear of being ridiculed.

Celexa   See CITALOPRAM.

citalopram (Celexa)   A selective serotonin reuptake inhibitor prescribed for many types of anxiety disorders.

claustrophobia   Fear of enclosed or confined spaces or being trapped.

clomipramine (Anafranil)   A tricyclic antidepressant specifically approved for the treatment of obsessive-compulsive disorder in children and sometimes prescribed for other types of anxiety disorders.

cognition   The process of knowing, recognizing, interpreting, judging, and reasoning.

cognitive   The process of knowing in the broadest sense, including perception, memory, and judgment.

cognitive-behavioral perspective   A theoretical approach to understanding behavior that focuses on how a person's thoughts and behavior are related to each other and how thoughts can become distorted and contribute to problem behavior.

cognitive-behavioral therapy (CBT)   A type of therapy focusing on specific therapy techniques used to change thoughts and behavior.

cognitive restructuring   A cognitive behavioral technique in which distorted thoughts or beliefs are evaluated so as to change behavior.

cognitive retraining   Developing or relearning the processes involved in thinking.

cognitive therapy   A form of psychotherapy based on the idea that emotional disorders are accompanied by distorted thought patterns that can be changed.

combat exhaustion   An obsolete name for post-traumatic stress disorder.

compulsions   Repetitive behaviors performed over and over again in response to an obsessive thought (usually a fear) as a way of temporarily easing anxiety.

compulsive   A term used to describe behaviors that are driven by anxiety.

coping strategies   Techniques that people use to cope with stress; the ability to deal with problems by attempting to overcome them or accept them.

cortisol   A hormone produced by the adrenal gland that increases during periods of stress; chronically high cortisol levels are associated with depression and anxiety.

cynophobia   Fear of dogs or rabies.

dentophobia   Fear of dentists.

doraphobia   Fear of fur or skins of animals.

dysphoria   An emotional state in which a person feels anxious or depressed.

elurophobia   See AILUROPHOBIA.

environmental stressors   Situations or events in the environment, such as work, school, crowds, relationships, or noise, that cause stress.

epinephrine (also adrenaline)   A hormone and neurotransmitter secreted by the adrenal gland during periods of stress that triggers a variety of changes in the body, including a rise in blood sugar and blood pressure; high levels of epinephrine have been associated with anxiety and panic attacks.

ereuthrophobia   Fear of blushing.

escitalopram (Lexapro)   A selective serotonin reuptake inhibitor prescribed for many types of anxiety disorders.

exposure therapy   A type of treatment for anxiety in which the patient is introduced to a feared object or situation, so he or she can learn that the object or situation can be faced without something bad happening.

family therapy   A type of treatment in which a patient and his or her family are treated together.

felinophobia   See AILUROPHOBIA.

flooding   An intense form of exposure therapy in which a person's anxiety is reduced by sudden, intense exposure to the source of anxiety.

fluoxetine (Prozac)   A selective serotonin reuptake inhibitor specifically approved for the treatment of obsessive-compulsive disorder in children, sometimes prescribed for other types of anxiety disorders.

fluvoxamine (Luvox)   A selective serotonin reuptake inhibitor specifically approved for the treatment of obsessive-compulsive disorder in children, sometimes prescribed for other types of anxiety disorders.

GABA   See GAMMA-AMINO BUTYRIC ACID.

galeophobia   See AILUROPHOBIA.

gamma-amino butyric acid (GABA)   A type of brain chemical called a neurotransmitter, which is linked to anxiety.

gatophobia   See AILUROPHOBIA.

generalized anxiety disorder (GAD)   An anxiety disorder characterized by chronic excessive and persistent worry about a number of issues, such as family, health, or finances, in the absence of a true threat.

hagiophobia   Fear of saints or holy things.

hematophobia (also hemophobia)   Fear of blood.

hemophobia   See HEMATOPHOBIA.

heterophobia   Fear of the opposite sex.

housebound   The inability to leave the house, a symptom common in severe cases of panic, agoraphobia, obsessive-compulsive disorder, and occasionally social phobia.

hydrophobia   Fear of water.

hydrophobophobia   Fear of rabies.

hypervigilance   Extreme sensitivity and constant scanning of the environment in searching for the presence of a feared object or situation.

hypsiphobia   See ACROPHOBIA.

Lexapro   See ESCITALOPRAM.

Luvox   See FLUVOXAMINE.

MAOIs   See MONOAMINE OXIDASE INHIBITORS.

melissophobia   See APIPHOBIA.

misophobia (or mysophobia)   Fear of being contaminated with dirt or germs.

mysophobia   See MISOPHOBIA.

monoamine oxidase inhibitors   Strong antidepressants thought to regulate chemicals in the central nervous system that may be used to treat anxiety disorders; they are rarely the first choice because they may interact dangerously with many other medications, foods, and beverages.

needlephobia See BELONEPHOBIA.

neuron A nerve cell.

neuropsychological examination A series of tasks that allow observation of performance presumed to be related to brain function.

neurosis A disorder characterized by anxiety or exaggerated avoidance of anxiety; a neurotic person understands that this behavior is not normal.

neurotransmitter A chemical substance that transmits information from one neuron to another.

noradrenaline (also norepinephrine) A hormone and neurotransmitter produced by the adrenal gland.

norepinephrine See NORADRENALINE.

neurotransmitter A chemical released by nerve cell endings that can transmit impulses across the space between nerve cells.

nyctophobia See ACHLUOPHOBIA.

obsessions Persistent and recurrent intrusive, disturbing thoughts, impulses, or images that a person cannot suppress or control.

obsessive A term used to describe persistent, intrusive, and recurrent unwanted thoughts, images, or impulses.

obsessive-compulsive disorder (OCD) An anxiety disorder characterized by persistent, intrusive, and recurrent unwanted thoughts that trigger uncontrollable behaviors, called compulsions, performed to control the anxiety triggered by the obsessions.

obsessive-compulsive personality A personality style characterized by concern with maintaining order, control, and following the rules.

obsessive-compulsive (OC) spectrum disorders A diverse group of problems that some experts believe may be related to obsessive-compulsive disorder, including compulsive gambling, trichotillomania, body dysmorphic disorder, hypochondriasis, somatization disorder, Tourette syndrome, autism, Asperger's syndrome, kleptomania, eating disorders, and other disorders of impulse control.

obsessive disorder A disorder characterized by persistent and recurrent unwanted thoughts, images, or impulses but few or no compulsions.

oneirophobia   Fear of dreams.

ophidiophobia   Fear of snakes.

ornithophobia   Fear of birds.

palpitations   An abnormally rapid heartbeat

panic   The basic emotion of fear that activates the fight-or-flight response; excessive, chronic panic in the absence of real danger is a characteristic of panic disorder.

panic attack   An episode of panic that represents an extreme form of the fear response.

panic disorder   An anxiety disorder characterized by recurring unexpected panic attacks in the absence of real danger.

paroxetine (Paxil)   A selective serotonin reuptake inhibitor prescribed for many types of anxiety disorders.

pathophobia   Fear of disease.

Paxil   See PAROXETINE.

performance anxiety   A fear of performing in front of other people, such as speaking in public, using the telephone, working, writing, eating, or drinking in front of others.

phasmophobia   Fear of ghosts.

phobia   An exaggerated fear of a particular object or situation.

photophobia   Fear of light.

post-traumatic stress disorder (PTSD)   An anxiety disorder following exposure to a traumatic event.

progressive muscle relaxation   A method of relaxation in which individual muscle groups are systematically tensed and relaxed; it can be used to ease symptoms of anxiety.

Prozac   See FLUOXETINE.

pteromerhanophobia   See AVIATOPHOBIA.

pyrophobia   Fear of fire.

rebound   The return of symptoms after treatment ends.

relaxation technique   Techniques such as breathing exercises, meditation, and yoga that are used to relax and ease symptoms of anxiety.

school phobia   An anxiety disorder characterized by inappropriate fear of going to school, often representing a dependency problem that is reinforced by attention from parents.

scriptophobia   Fear of writing in public.

selective mutism   A refusal to speak in specific social situations, such as at school, in which people would expect you to speak.

selective serotonin reuptake inhibitors (SSRIs)   A class of antidepressants that are used to treat some types of anxiety disorders and that work by boosting the amount of serotonin in the brain.

separation anxiety disorder　Excessive anxiety about being separated from home, from parents, or from other caregivers to whom a child is attached.

serotonin　A brain chemical linked to mood; low levels of serotonin are believed to trigger symptoms of depressed mood, anxiety, panic, or obsessions and compulsions.

sertraline (Zoloft)　A selective serotonin reuptake inhibitor specifically approved for the treatment of obsessive-compulsive disorder in children, also prescribed for many other types of anxiety disorders.

social phobia　A condition, sometimes called social anxiety disorder, characterized by a persistent and exaggerated fear of social situations because of fear of humiliation, embarrassment, rejection, and being observed.

spheksophobia　Fear of wasps.

SSRIs　See SELECTIVE SEROTONIN REUPTAKE INHIBITORS.

status panicus　A series of panic attacks that can last for hours or days.

stress-inoculation training　A type of psychotherapy that focuses on teaching techniques a person can use to cope with distorted thoughts and stress.

stressor　A situation or thought that leads to stress.

TCAs　See TRICYCLIC ANTIDEPRESSANTS.

trichotillomania　Compulsive hair pulling.

tricyclic antidepressants (TCAs)　A class of antidepressants that may be used to treat some anxiety disorders, thought to work by regulating several neurotransmitters.

tropophobia　Fear of moving or making changes.

trypanophobia　Fear of injections.

venlafaxine (Effexor)　A selective norepinephrine reuptake inhibitor (SNRI)—a type of antidepressant used to treat anxiety and depression disorders.

virtual reality exposure therapy　A type of exposure therapy in which artificial situations are presented to produce sensory experiences similar to actual feared situations.

Wellbutrin　See BUPROPRION.

withdrawal symptoms　Symptoms such as tremor, sweating, vomiting, insomnia, muscle pain, anxiety, and convulsions that occur after a drug that causes physical dependence is suddenly stopped.

Xanax See ALPRAZOLAM.

xenophobia A person unduly fearful or contemptuous of that which is foreign, especially of strangers or foreign peoples.

Zoloft See SERTRALINE.

zoophobia An abnormal and persistent fear of animals.

READ MORE ABOUT IT

ANXIETY DISORDERS

Beck, Aaron T., Gary Emery, and Ruth L. Greenberg. *Anxiety Disorders and Phobias: A Cognitive Perspective.* New York: Basic Books, 2005.

Bourne, Edmund J. *The Anxiety & Phobia Workbook,* 4th ed. Oakland, Calif.: New Harbinger Publications, 2005.

———. *Beyond Anxiety and Phobia: A Step-By-Step Guide to Lifetime Recovery.* Oakland, Calif.: New Harbinger Publications, 2001.

Chansky, Tamar E. *Freeing Your Child from Anxiety: Powerful, Practical Solutions to Overcome Your Child's Fears, Worries, and Phobias.* New York: Broadway, 2004.

Foxman, Paul. *The Worried Child: Recognizing Anxiety in Children and Helping Them Heal.* Alameda, Calif.: Hunter House Publishers, 2004.

Garber, Stephen W., Marianne Daniels Garber, and Robyn Freedman Spizman. *Monsters under the Bed and Other Childhood Fears: Helping Your Child Overcome Anxieties, Fears, and Phobias.* New York: Villard, 1993.

Marks, Isaac Meyer. *Fears, Phobias, and Rituals: Panic, Anxiety, and Their Disorders.* New York: Oxford University Press, 1987.

Marra, Thomas. *Depressed and Anxious: The Dialectical Behavior Therapy Workbook for Overcoming Depression and Anxiety.* Oakland, Calif.: New Harbinger Publications, 2004.

Peurifoy, Reneau Z. *Anxiety, Phobias, and Panic: A Step-by-Step Program for Regaining Control of Your Life.* Rev. ed. New York: Warner Books, 2005.

Seligman, Martin E. *The Optimistic Child: Proven Program to Safeguard Children from Depression and Build Lifelong Resilience.* New York: HarperCollins, 1996.

Smith, Laura L., and Charles Elliott. *Overcoming Anxiety for Dummies.* New York: Wiley, 2003.

Spence, Sue, Vanessa Cobham, Ann Wignall, and Ronald M. Rapee. *Helping Your Anxious Child: A Step-by-Step Guide for Parents.* Oakland, Calif.: New Harbinger Publications, 2000.

Spencer, Elizabeth DuPont, Robert L. DuPont, and Caroline M. DuPont. *The Anxiety Cure for Kids: A Guide for Parents.* New York: Wiley & Sons, 2003.

Strauss, Claudia J. *Talking to Anxiety: Simple Ways to Support Someone in Your LIfe Who Suffers from Anxiety.* New York: NAL Trade, 2004.

Wiederhold, Brenda K. *Conquering Panic, Anxiety, and Phobias: Achieving Success through Virtual Reality and Cognitive-Behavioral Therapy.* San Diego: Virtual Reality Medical Center Publications, 2004.

GENERALIZED ANXIETY DISORDER

Heimberg, Richard G. *Generalized Anxiety Disorder: Advances in Research and Practice.* New York: Guilford Press, 2004.

Rygh, Jayne L., and William C. Sanderson. *Treating Generalized Anxiety Disorder: Evidence-Based Strategies, Tools, and Techniques.* New York: Guilford Press, 2004.

White, John R. *Overcoming Generalized Anxiety Disorder—Client Manual: A Relaxation, Cognitive Restructuring, and Exposure-Based Protocol for the Treatment of GAD.* Best Practices for Therapy. Oakland, Calif.: New Harbinger Publications, 1999.

GENERAL TREATMENT OVERVIEW

Beck, Judith S. *Cognitive Therapy: Basics and Beyond.* New York: Guilford Press, 1995.

Bemis, Judith. *Embracing the Fear: Learning to Manage Anxiety and Panic Attacks.* Twin Cities, Minn.: Hazelden, 1994.

Bourne, Edmund J. *Coping with Anxiety: 10 Simple Ways to Relieve Anxiety, Fear, and Worry.* Oakland, Calif.: New Harbinger Publications, 2003.

Bourne, Edmund J., Arlen Brownstein, and Lorno Garlano. *Natural Relief for Anxiety: Complementary Strategies for Easing Fear, Panic and Worry.* Oakland, Calif.: New Harbinger Publications, 2004.

Burns, David D. *The Feeling Good Handbook.* New York: Plume, 1999.

Greenberger, Dennis. *Mind over Mood: Change How You Feel by Changing the Way You Think.* New York: Guilford Press, 1995.

INSPIRATION FOR TEENS

Carlson, Richard. *Don't Sweat the Small Stuff for Teens.* New York: Hyperion, 2000.

Covey, Sean. *Daily Reflections for Highly Effective Teens.* New York: Fireside, 1999.

Covey, Stephen R., and Sean Covey. *The Seven Habits of Highly Effective Teens Workbook.* The Seven Habits. Salt Lake City: Franklin Covey, 1999.

Friel, John C., and Linda Friel. *The Seven Best Things Smart Teens Do.* Deerfield Beach, Fla.: Health Communications, 2000.

Graham, Stedman. *Teens Can Make It Happen: Nine Steps for Success.* New York: Fireside, 2000.

OBSESSIVE-COMPULSIVE DISORDER

Baer, Lee. *Getting Control: Overcoming Your Obsessions and Compulsions.* New York: Plume, 2000.

Chansky, Tamar E. *Freeing Your Child from Obsessive-Compulsive Disorder: A Powerful, Practical Program for Parents of Children and Adolescents.* New York: Three Rivers Press, 2001.

De Silva, Padmal, and Stanley Rachman. *Obsessive Compulsive Disorders: The Facts.* New York: Oxford University Press, 1998.

Dumont, Raeann. *The Sky Is Falling: Understanding and Coping with Phobias, Panic, and Obsessive-Compulsive Disorders.* New York: W. W. Norton, 1997.

Foa, Edna. *Stop Obsessing!: How to Overcome Your Obsessions and Compulsions.* New York: Bantam Books, 2001.

Grayson, Jonathan. *Freedom from Obsessive Compulsive Disorder: A Personalized Recovery Program for Living with Uncertainty.* New York: Berkley Trade, 2004.

Landsman, Karen J. *Loving Someone with OCD: Help for You and Your Family.* Oakland, Calif.: New Harbinger Publications, 2005.

Maran, Linda. *Confronting the Bully of OCD: Winning Back Our Freedom One Day at a Time.* Brooklyn: Fifteenth Street Publishing, 2004.

March, John S. *OCD in Children and Adolescents: A Cognitive-Behavioral Treatment Manual.* New York: Guilford Press, 1998.

Niner, Holly L. *Mr. Worry: A Story about OCD.* Morton Grove, Ill.: Albert Whitman & Company, 2004.

Osborn, Ian. *Tormenting Thoughts and Secret Rituals: The Hidden Epidemic of Obsessive-Compulsive Disorder.* New York: Dell, 1999.

Penzel, Fred. *Obsessive-Compulsive Disorders: A Complete Guide to Getting Well and Staying Well.* New York: Oxford University Press, 2000.

Schwartz, Jeffrey M. *Brain Lock: Free Yourself from Obsessive-Compulsive Behavior.* New York: HarperCollins, 1997.

Shackman, Lynn, and Shelagh Masline. *Why Does Everything Have to Be Perfect? Understanding Obsessive-Compulsive Disorder.* New York: Dell, 1999.

Wagner, Aureen Pinto. *Up and Down the Worry Hill: A Childrens Book about Obsessive-Compulsive Disorder and Its Treatment.* New York: Lighthouse Press, 2004.

PANIC

Antony, Martin M., and Randi McCabe. *10 Simple Solutions to Panic: How to Overcome Panic Attacks, Calm Physical Symptoms, and Reclaim Your Life.* Oakland, Calif.: New Harbinger, 2004.

Babior, Shirley, and Carol Goldman. *Overcoming Panic, Anxiety, and Phobias: New Strategies to Free Yourself from Worry and Fear.* Duluth, Minn.: Whole Person Associates, 1996.

Bassett, Lucinda. *From Panic to Power: Proven Techniques to Calm Your Anxieties, Conquer Your Fears, and Put You in Control of Your Life.* New York: HarperResource, 1997.

Bemis, Judith. *Embracing the Fear: Learning to Manage Anxiety and Panic Attacks.* Twin Cities, Minn.: Hazelden, 1994.

Carbonell, David. *Panic Attacks Workbook: A Guided Program for Beating the Panic Trick.* Berkeley, Calif.: Ulysses Press, 2004.

Dumont, Raeann. *The Sky Is Falling: Understanding and Coping with Phobias, Panic, and Obsessive-Compulsive Disorders.* New York: W. W. Norton, 1997.

Feniger, Mani. *Journey from Anxiety to Freedom: Moving beyond Panic and Phobias and Learning to Trust Yourself.* Roseville, Calif.: Prima Lifestyles, 1997.

Glatzer, Jenna, and Paul Foxman. *Conquering Panic and Anxiety Disorders: Success Stories, Strategies, and Other Good News.* Alameda, Calif.: Hunter House Publishers, 2002.

Granoff, Abbot Lee. *Help! I Think I'm Dying! Panic Attacks and Phobias: A Consumer's Guide.* Norfolk, Va.: Mind Matters, 1999.

Handly, Robert. *Anxiety and Panic Attacks: Their Cause and Cure.* New York: Fawcett, 1987.

Marks, Isaac Meyer. *Fears, Phobias, and Rituals: Panic, Anxiety, and Their Disorders.* New York: Oxford University Press, 1987.

Peurifoy, Reneau Z. *Anxiety, Phobias, and Panic: A Step-by-Step Program for Regaining Control of Your Life.* Rev. ed. New York: Warner Books, 2005.

Ross, Jerilyn. *Triumph over Fear: A Book of Help and Hope for People.* New York: Bantam, 1995.

Silove, Derrick. *Overcoming Panic: A Self-Help Guide Using Cognitive Behavioral Techniques.* New York: New York University Press, 2001.

Swede, Shirley, and Jaffe, Seymour. *The Panic Attack Recovery Book.* New York: New American Library, 2000.

Weekes, Claire. *Hope and Help for Your Nerves.* New York: Signet Book, 1991.

Weinstock, Lorna, and Eleanor Gilman. *Overcoming Panic Disorder.* New York: McGraw-Hill, 1998.

Wiederhold, Brenda K. *Conquering Panic, Anxiety, and Phobias: Achieving Success through Virtual Reality and Cognitive-Behavioral Therapy.* San Diego: Virtual Reality Medical Center Publications, 2004.

Wilson, R. Reid. *Don't Panic, Revised Edition: Taking Control of Anxiety Attacks.* New York: Collins, 1996.

PHOBIAS

Antony, Martin M., and Randi McCabe. *Overcoming Animal and Insect Phobias: How to Conquer Fear of Dogs, Snakes, Rodents, Bees, Spiders and More.* Oakland, Calif.: New Harbinger Publications, 2005.

Babior, Shirley, and Carol Goldman. *Overcoming Panic, Anxiety, and Phobias: New Strategies to Free Yourself from Worry and Fear.* Duluth, Minn.: Whole Person Associates, 1996.

Beck, Aaron T., Gary Emery, and Ruth L. Greenberg. *Anxiety Disorders and Phobias: A Cognitive Perspective.* New York: Basic Books, 2005.

Beidel, Deborah, and Samuel Turner. *Shy Children, Phobic Adults: Nature and Treatment of Social Phobia.* Washington, D.C.: American Psychological Association, 1997.

Bourne, Edmund J. *The Anxiety and Phobia Workbook.* 4th ed. Oakland, Calif.: New Harbinger Publications, 2005.

———. *Beyond Anxiety and Phobia: A Step-by-Step Guide to Lifetime Recovery.* Oakland, Calif.: New Harbinger Publications, 2001.

Burns, Marilyn. *Math: Facing an American Phobia.* Sausalito, Calif.: Math Solutions Publications, 1998.

Csoti, Marianna. *School Phobia, Panic Attacks, and Anxiety in Children.* London: Jessica Kingsley Publishers, 2003.

Dumont, Raeann. *The Sky Is Falling: Understanding and Coping with Phobias, Panic, and Obsessive-Compulsive Disorders.* New York: W. W. Norton, 1997.

Feniger, Mani. *Journey from Anxiety to Freedom: Moving beyond Panic and Phobias and Learning to Trust Yourself.* Roseville, Calif.: Prima Lifestyles, 1997.

Garber, Stephen W., Marianne Daniels Garber, and Robyn Freedman Spizman. *Monsters under the Bed and Other Childhood Fears: Helping Your Child Overcome Anxieties, Fears, and Phobias.* New York: Villard, 1993.

Gardner, James, and Arthur H. Bell. *Phobias and How to Overcome Them: Understanding and Beating Your Fears.* New York: New Page Books, 2005.

Granoff, Abbot Lee. *Help! I Think I'm Dying! Panic Attacks and Phobias: A Consumer's Guide.* Norfolk, Va.: Mind Matters, 1999.

Greenberg, Gary. *The Pop-Up Book of Phobias.* New York: HarperCollins, 1999.

Kahn, Ada P., and Ronald M. Doctor. *Phobias (Life Balance).* New York: Scholastic, 2003.

Lipsman, Ron. *You Can Do the Math: Overcome Your Math Phobia and Make Better Financial Decisions.* Westport, Conn.: Praeger Publishers, 2004.

Marks, Isaac Meyer. *Fears, Phobias, and Rituals: Panic, Anxiety, and Their Disorders.* New York: Oxford University Press, 1987.

McCullough, Leigh, Amelia Kaplan, Stuart Andrews, et al. *Treating Affect Phobia: A Manual for Short-Term Dynamic Psychotherapy.* New York: Guilford Press, 2003.

Northrup, Christie. *Hanging Up on Your Phone Phobias.* New York: CAN-net Consulting, 2004.

Peurifoy, Reneau Z. *Anxiety, Phobias, and Panic: A Step-by-Step Program for Regaining Control of Your Life.* Rev. ed. New York: Warner Books, 2005.

Waters, Richard. *Phobias: Revealed and Explained.* New York: Barron's Educational Series, 2004.

Wiederhold, Brenda K. *Conquering Panic, Anxiety, and Phobias: Achieving Success through Virtual Reality and Cognitive-Behavioral Therapy.* San Diego: Virtual Reality Medical Center Publications, 2004.

Young, Ed. *Know Fear: Facing Life's Six Most Common Phobias.* Nashville: Broadman & Holman Publishers, 2003.

POST-TRAUMATIC STRESS DISORDER

Herman, Judith. *Trauma and Recovery: The Aftermath of Violence—from Domestic Abuse to Political Terror.* New York: Basic Books, 1997.

Matsakis, Aphrodite. *I Can't Get Over It: A Handbook for Trauma Survivors.* Oakland, Calif.: New Harbinger Publications, 1996.

———. *Trust after Trauma: A Guide to Relationships for Survivors and Those Who Love Them.* Oakland, Calif.: New Harbinger Publications, 1998.

Rosenbloom, Dena. *Life after Trauma: A Workbook for Healing.* New York: Guilford Press, 1999.

Schiraldi, Glenn R. *Post-Traumatic Stress Disorder Sourcebook.* New York: McGraw-Hill, 2000.

Smyth, Larry. *Overcoming Post-Traumatic Stress Disorder—Client Manual.* Best Practices: Empirically Based Treatment Protocols Series. Oakland, Calif.: New Harbinger Publications. June, 1999.

Williams, Mary Beth, and Soili Poijula. *The PTSD Workbook: Simple, Effective Techniques for Overcoming Traumatic Stress Symptoms.* Oakland, Calif.: New Harbinger Publications, 2002.

RELAXATION TECHNIQUES

Blumenfield, Larry. *The Big Book of Relaxation: Simple Techniques to Control the Excess Stress in Your Life.* Broomfield, Colo.: Relaxation Co., 1994.

Brantley, Jeffrey. *Calming Your Anxious Mind: How Mindfulness and Compassion Can Free You from Anxiety, Fear, and Panic.* Oakland, Calif.: New Harbinger Publications, 2003.

Davich, Victor N. *The Best Guide to Meditation.* New York: Renaissance Books, 1998.

———. *Minute Meditation: Quiet Your Mind. Change Your Life.* New York: Perigee Books, 2004.

Davis, Martha, Matthew McKay, and Elizabeth Robbins Eshelman. *The Relaxation and Stress Reduction Workbook.* Oakland, Calif.: New Harbinger Publications, 2000.

Elkin, Allen. *Stress Management for Dummies.* Foster City, Calif.: IDG Books, 1999.

Farhi, Donna. *The Breathing Book: Vitality and Good Health through Essential Breath Work.* New York: Owl Books, 1996.

Hendricks, Gay. *Conscious Breathing: Breathwork for Health, Stress Release, and Personal Mastery.* New York: Bantam, 1995.

Kabat-Zinn, Jon. *Wherever You Go, There You Are: Mindfulness Meditation in Everyday Life.* New York: Hyperion, 1995.

Kennerley, Helen. *Overcoming Anxiety: A Self-Help Guide Using Cognitive Behavioral Techniques.* New York: New York University Press, 1997.

Lazarus, Judith. *Stress Relief and Relaxation Techniques.* New York: McGraw-Hill, 2000.

Lewis, Dennis. *Free Your Breath, Free Your Life: How Conscious Breathing Can Relieve Stress, Increase Vitality, and Help You Live More Fully.* Boston: Shambhala, 2004.

Leyden-Rubenstein, Lori. *The Stress Management Handbook.* New Canaan, Conn.: Keats Publishing, 1998.

Lite, Lori. *A Boy and a Bear: The Children's Relaxation Book.* North Branch, Minn.: Specialty Press, 1996.

Payne, Rosemary A. *Relaxation Techniques: A Practical Handbook for the Health Care Professional.* New York: Churchill Livingstone, 2000.

Rubin, Manning. *Ways to Relieve Stress in 60 Seconds.* New York: Workman Publishing, 1993.

Schiffmann, Erich. *Yoga: The Spirit and Practice of Moving into Stillness.* New York: Pocket, 1996.

Speads, Carola. *Ways to Better Breathing.* Rochester, Vt.: Healing Arts Press, 1992.

Wilson, Paul. *Instant Calm: Over 100 Easy-to-Use Techniques for Relaxing Mind and Body.* New York: Plume, 1995.

Zi, Nancy. *The Art of Breathing: Six Simple Lessons to Improve Performance, Health, and Well-Being.* Berkeley, Calif.: North Atlantic Books, 2000.

SHYNESS AND SOCIAL PHOBIA

Antony, Martin M. *The Shyness and Social Anxiety Workbook: Proven Techniques for Overcoming Your Fears.* Oakland, Calif.: New Harbinger Publications, 2000.

Beidel, Deborah, and Samuel Turner. *Shy Children, Phobic Adults: Nature and Treatment of Social Phobia.* Washington, D.C.: American Psychological Association, 1997.

Berent, Jonathan, and Amy Lemley. *Beyond Shyness: How to Conquer Social Anxieties.* New York: Fireside, 1994.

Boothman, Nicholas. *How to Make People Like You in 90 Seconds or Less.* New York: Workman Publishing Company, 2000.

Capps, Donald. *Social Phobia: Alleviating Anxiety in an Age of Self-Promotion.* Nashville, Tenn.: Chalice Press, 1999.

Carducci, Bernardo J. *The Pocket Guide to Making Successful Small Talk: How to Talk to Anyone Anytime Anywhere about Anything.* New York: Pocket Guide Company, 1999.

Carducci, Bernardo J., and Susan Golant. *Shyness: A Bold New Approach.* New York: Harper, 2000.

Dayhoff, Signe A. *Diagonally-Parked in a Parallel Universe: Working Through Social Anxiety.* Placitas, N.Mex.: Effectiveness-Plus Publications, 2000.

Gabor, Don. *How to Start a Conversation and Make Friends.* New York: Fireside, 2001.

Garner, Alan. *Conversationally Speaking: Tested New Ways to Increase Your Personal and Social Effectiveness.* New York: McGraw-Hill, 1997.

Heimberg, Richard G., and Robert E. Becker. *Cognitive-Behavioral Group Therapy for Social Phobia: Basic Mechanisms and Clinical Strategies.* New York: Guildford Press, 1995.

Heimberg, Richard G., Michael R. Liebowitz, Debra A. Hope, and Franklin R. Schneier, eds. *Social Phobia: Diagnosis, Assessment, and Treatment.* New York: Guildford Press, 1995.

Hofmann, Stefan G., and Patricia Marten DiBartolo. *From Social Anxiety to Social Phobia: Multiple Perspectives.* New York: Allyn & Bacon, 2000.

Markway, Barbara G., Cheryl Carmin, C. Alec Pollard, and Teresa Flynn. *Dying of Embarrassment: Help for Social Anxiety and Phobia.* Oakland, Calif.: New Harbinger Publications, 1992.

Markway, Barbara, and Gregory Markway. *Painfully Shy: How to Overcome Social Anxiety and Reclaim Your Life.* New York: St. Martin's/ Griffin, 2003.

Marshall, John R. *Social Phobia: From Shyness to Stage Fright.* New York: Basic Books, 1995.

Martinet, Jeanne. *The Art of Mingling: Easy, Proven Techniques for Mastering Any Room.* New York: St. Martin's, 1992.

Rapee, Ronald M. *Overcoming Shyness and Social Phobia: A Step-by-Step Guide.* Clinical Application of Evidence-Based Psychotherapy. Lanham, Md.: Jason Aronson, 1998.

RoAne, Susan. *How to Work a Room: The Ultimate Guide to Savvy Socializing in Person and Online.* New York: HarperCollins, 2000.

———. *What Do I Say Next? Talking Your Way to Business and Social Success.* New York: Warner Books, 1999.

Schmidt, Louis A., and Jay Schulkin, eds. *Extreme Fear, Shyness, and Social Phobia: Origins, Biological Mechanisms, and Clinical Outcomes.* Series in Affective Science. New York: Oxford University Press, 1999.

INDEX